Forgotten Conscripts

Forgotten Conscripts

Understanding the Needs of Military-Connected Adolescents

Jennie L. Hanna

ROWMAN & LITTLEFIELD
Lanham • Boulder • New York • London

Published by Rowman & Littlefield
An imprint of The Rowman & Littlefield Publishing Group, Inc.
4501 Forbes Boulevard, Suite 200, Lanham, Maryland 20706
www.rowman.com

86-90 Paul Street, London EC2A 4NE, United Kingdom

Copyright © 2022 by Jennie L. Hanna

All rights reserved. No part of this book may be reproduced in any form or by any electronic or mechanical means, including information storage and retrieval systems, without written permission from the publisher, except by a reviewer who may quote passages in a review.

British Library Cataloguing in Publication Information Available

Library of Congress Cataloging-in-Publication Data Available

ISBN 9781475860955 (cloth : alk. paper) | ISBN 9781475860962 (pbk. : alk. paper) | ISBN 9781475860979 (ebook)

*For Chris and Christopher,
who will always be my favorite soldiers,
and for David,
who was the military-connected adolescent
I always pictured when I wrote.*

Contents

Acknowledgments	ix
Introduction	xi
Chapter 1: Life within the Military Culture	1
Chapter 2: The Identity of the Forgotten Conscript	15
Chapter 3: High Expectations for Forgotten Conscripts	25
Chapter 4: The Burdens of Being the New Kid	33
Chapter 5: Deployment and Reunification of the Military Family	41
Chapter 6: Advantages and Aggravations within the Military Culture	53
Chapter 7: Coping Strategies for Forgotten Conscripts	63
Chapter 8: The Lasting Impact of Growing Up Military	73
Chapter 9: Implications for Educators of Forgotten Conscripts	81
Glossary of Common Military Terms and Acronyms	89
References	97
About the Author	101

Acknowledgments

A journey like this can only be achieved through the support of others. Thankfully, I was surrounded by a sea of them.

To my family, near and far, thank you for being my loudest cheerleaders and for not rolling your eyes when all I could talk about was military children and research for the past several years. To my husband, Chris, who could sense when I was taking on too much before I could, thank you for reminding me to take care of myself first and being there to do it when you knew I wouldn't. To my son, Christopher, thank you for showing how proud you are of me—I hope I continue to make you as proud as you have made me as you are set to embark on your own journey as a soldier. To my mother, Teresa, thank you for being my honest sounding board. You will never know how much I will treasure those conversations. To my father, Hal, who gave me my first foray into the military life, thank you for being a role model for just how far persistence can take a person and for blessing me with my ability to write.

I also need to thank Dr. Lawrence Baines for your guidance and patience through my doubt, myriad of questions, and long-winded drafts of this research. Your faith in me was always there when I needed it. That and your handy ink pen.

Finally, to the nine military-connected adolescents featured in this book, I am grateful for the faith and confidence you showed when you agreed to open yourself up and share your life with me and the rest of the world. The life of a military child is not an easy one and revisiting old wounds took courage, so for that, I will always be grateful. Hopefully, your sacrifice will make it easier to cultivate support for fellow military brats in the future—lord knows you all deserve it.

Introduction

Adolescents all yearn to be seen. It is only to what extent the sentiment varies.

A select few might seek the spotlight—to catch the eye of a current crush or to secure the top spot on the basketball team—while others are comfortable watching from the sidelines, hidden from the stares of others. A handful even wish to be immortalized at all costs—care to do a TikTok dance, anyone?

Yet despite our social media-driven world, there is a large portion of our community that by default lives a partially invisible existence throughout their formative years: *military-connected children and adolescents*.

Stanford University professor Deborah Stipek (2006) wrote that students' nonacademic needs are not only often overlooked but an essential piece school must seek to understand in hopes of meeting academic and social expectations. Factors like family structure, access to adequate healthcare, social-emotional well-being, and many others impact student success from the shadows.

Being able to meet these needs becomes exponentially harder when teachers are unaware of the full background of their students. It is like trying to put together a puzzle without realizing some key pieces are missing.

The family is a vital source of support within the military culture, often referred to as the backbone of the military itself. It is those left at home that keep the family together while the soldier heads full-on into battle. Yet unlike our all-volunteer armed forces, military-connected children didn't pick this life—they were *drafted* into it.

Simply put, military-connected adolescents are forgotten conscripts—compulsorily enlisted into service with the military-industrial complex, whether they wanted it or not.

To make matters even worse, forgotten conscripts watch as their contribution to supporting their soldier parents so they can focus on more pressing issues during conflict in war zones are overlooked or ignored.

The classroom is an ideal place to increase tolerance and diversity awareness. In general, children who are supported by a caring adult tend to thrive educationally, emotionally, and socially (Easterbrooks, Ginsburg & Lerner, 2013; Ginsburg & Jablow, 2006). Since schools are the closest communities and social networks outside the home, it is necessary to find ways to help military-connected students feel seen.

Public perception is that most forgotten conscripts attend Department of Defense schools, but that is not reality. Over four million military-connected children in the U.S.—80% of which attend public schools resulting in at least one military-connected child in every school district in the nation (De Pedro et al., 2018; Lester & Flake, 2013). Classrooms and teachers can and must play a key role in helping to support these adolescents.

But that can only happen if educators are aware of the presence of forgotten conscripts in their classrooms.

Every teacher in the United States is an educator of military-connected children. Even if the family is no longer serving in an active capacity, the beliefs, expectations, and traditions of this culture are pervasive. They endure and leave an indelible mark on all members long after the soldier parent is no longer a part of Uncle Sam's duty roster.

Unlike other marginalized groups, forgotten conscripts do not display outward markers of their membership within the military culture. There is no common accent to their speech or gait in their walk. To the untrained eye, forgotten conscripts look and act just like any other civilian teenager.

Despite these high numbers, little is known about military-connected adolescents. In a nation that has been at war around the globe for decades, the notion that research is limited on how military kids see themselves in the world is unfathomable.

The nomadic life of a military-connected adolescent is hard enough without having to continually acclimate every few years because of a lack of understanding. At each new school, students encounter a dearth of educational awareness about military culture and the needs of military-connected adolescents in school settings. Hidden from the rest of the world is a lifetime of separation, transition, and learned resiliency.

Working to create a welcoming and supportive environment in educational spaces for military-connected adolescents can help support members of this community. Simply having this part of their identity recognized in education can help with building confidence and forming a sense of stability to make the difficult occurrences better.

Chapter 1 focuses on historical research concerning growing up military and the impact membership within this culture has on youth. Chapters 2–8 take a deeper dive into the identity development, strengths, stressors, and various experiences growing up amid the backdrop of the military culture. Chapter 9 will suggest implications for educators and administrators as they continue teaching and learning among this population. There is also a glossary of commonly used words and phrases within the military culture that those in education should know located at the back of the book.

Jordan (2002) asserts that these youth are active participants in a culture made up of experiences, networks, and relationships often unseen by "outsiders." As such, military-connected adolescents should not be viewed as victims of their circumstances but treated as the wellspring of knowledge about their feelings and encounters as they make the transition to adulthood. So, who better to ask what it is like to grow up as a part of this invisible minority than the forgotten conscripts themselves?

This is the driving force behind the research in this book.

Chapter 1

Life within the Military Culture

Military-connected adolescents live in our neighborhoods. They go to our schools and are members of the quintessential American family. There is much we can learn from them. Yet, despite the increase in service members over the years, there is surprisingly little research on military-connected adolescents, especially in terms of understanding who they are and how they perceive their place in the world.

Beginning around World War II, research on military-connected children was initiated for two purposes: 1) to look into the military family and 2) to understand how stress affects these families (McCubbin, Dahl & Hunter, 1976). While these are still important topics, just as war has changed for soldiers, the landscape and experiences among this population have evolved. Even studies conducted as recently as Operation Desert Storm in the early 1990s may not necessarily apply to the current population of military-connected children as recent conflicts in Iraq and Afghanistan since the early 2000s have proffered a continual wave of deployments throughout their formative years (Chartrand & Siegel, 2007).

The U.S. military consists of a multitude of different cultures, religions, races, and ethnicities, but it can also be considered a distinctive culture in its own right. As an often-unidentified culture within schools, Mmari et al. (2009) claims most educators are unaware of strategies to help support the social, emotional, and academic growth of the members of this invisible minority.

To address the needs of military-connected children, a Memorandum of Understanding (2008) between the U.S. Department of Defense and the Department of Education was developed. Designed as a "framework for collaboration," the objectives of the partnership were to increase efforts to support military-connected children in terms of the development of academic and coping skills to help support education, transition, and deployment issues (p. 1). President Obama took it a step further with a presidential directive to all federal agencies to make the education of military-connected children a top priority (Esqueda, Astor & De Pedro, 2012). Yet despite these steps, youth in this population remains on the fringe as one of the most invisible minorities in public education.

MILITARY FAMILIES

There is an unspoken understanding that when a soldier joins the military, their family also enlists for the cause (Park, 2011). It becomes abundantly clear early on to dependents that the mission of the military will always come first and the family second.

With 3.2 million personnel stationed in all 50 states and 150 countries worldwide, the United States armed forces is one of the largest employers in the world (McCarthy, 2015). Yet despite these high numbers, bearing the label of "part of a military family" remains an unstudied but important phenomenon (Kranke et al., 2019, p. 193).

The U.S. military consists of six service branches: Army, Navy, Air Force, Marines, and Coast Guard and the newly formed Space Force. Each branch of service has its own full-time or active-duty component along with a part-time or reserve section, both with the mission to fight for and protect the citizens of the United States of America. The Army and Air Force also have National Guard units, which have a dual duty to support at the national and state level.

When the government moved forward with an all-volunteer force in 1973, the military culture underwent a drastic makeover. More soldiers opt to serve not for a single enlistment but a full-blown career. Ranks of young, single soldiers were soon joined by more spouses and parents.

Whether it is a family tradition or a desire to serve their country, many also sign up because it is a secure source of employment. The military is a younger workforce when compared to other lifelong professions since many join right out of high school (Clever & Segal, 2013).

The subculture that families create because of their shared experiences within the military is as distinctive as any race or ethnicity within the larger population (Hall, 2011; Montalvo, 1976). Military families come in many different types including nuclear, single parent, blended, and multigenerational.

A growing number of soldiers are dual military, where both parents serve with the armed forces. During the Vietnam War, only 10% of the fighting force was married (Lester & Flake, 2013), but now more than 50% are married and 70% have at least one child (Huebner et al., 2009; Milburn & Lightfoot, 2013).

The age of military personnel (active duty, National Guard or Reserves, and civil service) typically ranges from 28 to 32 years old. More than 70% are white, non-Hispanic. 80% are male, and more than 90% have a high school degree or higher (Clever & Segal, 2013). Of female soldiers, 30% are mothers, while 7% of the fighting force are also single parents raising military-connected children alone (Lester & Flake, 2013).

Core values are unchanging foundational elements within a certain group or culture. They provide a sense of group identity and govern how people interact both within the organization and with others outside the group or culture. According to the Military Leadership Diversity Commission (2009), the Department of Defense emphasizes core values in all branches including duty, integrity, ethics, honor, courage, loyalty, leadership, and professionalism. Many of these values in turn become part of the fabric of the military-connected child via their upbringing with a military parent.

Some negative elements come with being a part of this population. Military families tend to be more authoritarian, while high mobility and parental deployments leave an indelible mark on military families. According to Thompson et al. (2017), most families thrive on predictable patterns to maintain homeostasis, so as military families face consistent moves or deployments, this threatens that stability, forcing them to adjust behaviors to adapt to the change and reestablish equilibrium.

The home parent, in this case often the mother, becomes an important figure in the military family as a touchstone, a source of stability, and go-between during a crisis. Despite the mother's central role, women tend to be less valued in the military—both as a military spouse and as a soldier—which, as Wertsch (1991) claims reinforces the patriarchal element embedded in the culture.

Certain types of military families have even higher risks for anxiety, poor academic performance, and depression. Those include young parents, foreign-born spouses, and those who are married to someone in the lower enlisted ranks (Park, 2011). While military life is already hard, these heighten those hardships.

Perils and problems are also more likely to occur among National Guard and Reservist families who are forced to adjust to serving in a full-time capacity as opposed to one weekend a month. Often the National Guard or Reserve soldiers live hundreds of miles away from the closest military installation, only increasing their sense of isolation. In fact, between 2001 to 2007, the Department of Defense mobilized more than 550,000 National Guard and Reservist soldiers—the greatest number since World War II (Baptist et al., 2015; Kranke et al., 2019).

MILITARY-CONNECTED CHILDREN

Wertsch (1991) reminds us that despite its pejorative connotation, military-connected children often use the self-imposed moniker *military brat* to show their membership within this culture. Military-connected children also subsume the "third culture kid" label as they find their identity formation influenced by formative years growing up immersed in other cultures, creating a "third" cultural identification (Pollock & Van Reken, 2009). No matter the term used, since there are little to no outward differences between military brats and civilians, recognition of their identity and their specific needs go unacknowledged, especially in education.

And the world is not lacking for forgotten conscripts. For every soldier serving, there are on average 1.4 military-connected children, with a larger percentage of elementary-aged youth or below, since soldiers tend to enlist for 10 years or less (Clever & Segal, 2013). Sherman and Glenn (2006) point out the only exception is among National Guardsmen and Reservists who often serve longer terms and thus tend to have older children.

Military-connected children face a wide array of adversities as a part of this population including isolation, low-socioeconomic status, parental absence, mission importance over family, and authoritarian culture. Because of the stress of mobility and deployment, some military-connected adolescents have problems with trust, attachment, and security that last long after their childhood days are done.

As a member of an invisible minority, the notion that military-connected children grow up among a culture defined by rigid discipline, nomadic rootlessness, dedication to the military mission, and the threat of war and personal loss, remains just below the surface. Difficulties are even more common for children of National Guard and Reserve soldiers, according to Baptist et al. (2015). These adolescents find themselves facing a major lifestyle change when suddenly thrust deeper into the military culture during parental deployments or tours of duty.

As a rule, soldiers are taught to hide emotions and to explicitly follow orders to prepare for combat. The problem arises when that same principle is applied at home, where they often have difficulty expressing love to even their family for fear of looking weak. As such, military-connected children can feel growing up that they are supposed to be seen and not heard and often perceive an expectation to wear masks of secrecy, stoicism, and even denial of fear, especially in front of the military parent (Wertsch, 1991).

There is also a pattern of behavior in terms of how boys and girls are raised in military families. Daughters are viewed as pretty things and doted on during their younger years but claim to feel invisible in the eyes of the military parent when they grow up (Wertsch, 1991, p. 94–95). The more authoritarian the parent, the more invisible the daughter becomes, making it harder to forge connections between her and her military parent, which can impact adolescent identity development into adulthood.

Many daughters feel the only way to be seen by the military parent is to either act out in rebellious and destructive ways or become more "seen" by joining the military service themselves. Daughters quickly learn that they remain invisible whether they rebel or conform, which can lead to control issues in their own life (Wertsch, 1991, p. 110, 118).

Sons, on the other hand, are *rarely* invisible in the military family, especially in the eyes of the military parent. This is apparent even more if they are first-born sons. According to Wertsch (1991), boys are held to higher standards, taught to be more aggressive, endure tougher punishments, suffer from less privacy than their sisters, feel unable to express any emotions other than aggression or anger, and often face rampant homophobia (p. 144–149).

Sons, whether they want to or not, often internalize the warrior spirit, feeling unable to pass up a dare or a fistfight, something that follows them into adulthood. Sports can provide an avenue for boys to release aggression, but involvement can be detrimental if the military parent looks at the hobby as a means to help toughen up his or her son. Many sons claim that the only ways to escape the military parent's eyes are when he is physically strong enough to best the parent or is old enough to finally move away (p. 154).

Issues of feeling a lack of control manifest themselves in different ways in male and female forgotten conscripts, where daughters tend to gravitate toward eating disorders and self-harming behaviors, and sons either take a passive stance on everything or become obsessive perfectionists throughout life. Whether the military-connected child is male or female, Wertsch (1991) claims those who come out as LGBTQ face difficulties with acceptance in the uber-masculine military culture (p. 177). This still endures today.

Pollock and Van Reken (2009) join military-connected children together with missionary, business, and expatriate children who all fit the definition of a third culture kid. Personal characteristics of third culture kids include:

1. adaptability, but lack of true cultural balance
2. the ability to blend in but a difficulty in defining individual differences
3. having fewer feelings of prejudice, but being more aware of it in the world
4. a focus on living in the now, but at the detriment of knowing they have no choice in the future at times and
5. an appreciation of authority, yet mistrustful of its intrusion (p. 99–110).

Two realities that apply to third culture kids across the board include being raised in genuinely cross-cultural and highly mobile worlds. Pollock and Van Reken (2009) developed the PolVan Cultural Identity Model, which looks at adolescent identity in two ways: the changing nature of how individuals relate to their surrounding culture and how their identity is constantly being redefined in contrast or comparison to whichever culture they are currently in (p. 54).

The PolVan Cultural Identity Model contains four sections: the *foreigner* who look different and think differently from the current culture, the *adopted* who look different but tend to think alike, the *mirror* who look alike and think alike, and the *hidden immigrant*—which include forgotten conscripts—who may look alike but think differently than the dominant culture.

Because of the distinctiveness of the military culture, most military-connected adolescents tend to seek each other out for friendship because of the comfortable understanding of the demands and expectations among military-connect children. Wertsch (1991) claims military-connected children develop special adaptations to help them survive and even thrive, including a special "antenna" to identify fellow military brats, the ability to mimic others to blend in, forced extroversion to help make new connections, a desire to travel light, and expertise in saying goodbye.

Since adolescent identity development is linked to the ability to develop strong interpersonal friendships, the high mobility of the military family makes identity development problematic for military-connected children, according to Williams and Mariglia (2002).

Learning to blend in amid the "new kid" label becomes a double-edged sword for military-connected youth because it may allow them to learn how to fit in and make friends quickly, yet, as McDonald (2010) points out, there is an unspoken urge to keep others at a distance to protect themselves from the potential pain that comes with moving. However, as Tyler (2002) illustrates, youth consistently emphasize that the military also serves as a source of support despite issues that come with being a part of the culture.

Military-connected adolescents endure difficulties as part of their transient upbringing. Each move to a new place forces them to change worldviews, expectations for behavior, and even languages at times. Pollock and Van Reken (2009) show that when reentering their home culture, these children often take on one of three roles:

1. the chameleon who mimics others in hopes of achieving peer acceptance,
2. the screamer who makes sure everyone is aware of how they are different,
3. the wallflower who just hopes to blend in and go undetected.

One should not misinterpret challenges as liabilities among forgotten conscripts, who often view obstacles as ways to better themselves and build resiliency. These youth know they are allowed an opportunity to experience the world in ways others can only do through books, movies, and the news.

MILITARY-CONNECTED ADOLESCENT STRESSORS

Like with all cultures, military life is too fluid to encapsulate into one set of characteristics. As the interloper in most situations, they live with an outsider identity, feeling they only fit within the margins. When forgotten conscripts start to believe their lives are normal, Atuel et al., (2011) posits that it only takes moving to a new post or the deployment of a loved one off to a war zone to bring them back to reality.

When trying to compare military-connected adolescent stressors with that of civilian children, Olsen (2012) claims it is useful to keep in mind that the sources of their obstacles come from vastly different places. This is not to discount the obstacles and hardships of civilian students, but rather that forgotten conscripts can experience those on top of the ones that come from growing up military.

Additionally, Bolton (2006) reminds stressors like high mobility, separation, and anxiety due to parental deployment, academic and school issues, and personal and cultural identity development issues are common among military-connected children of all ages.

HIGH MOBILITY

Military-connected children move to a new duty station an average of every three years, 2.4 times often more than civilians (Clever & Segal, 2013). The military family is impacted financially during these reoccurring relocations. Each move requires the nonmilitary spouse to secure new employment, resulting in a tumultuous work history, an inability to secure managerial positions, and subsequently earning up to 2% less in salary at each new duty station (Clever & Segal, 2013).

Keeping people at arm's length often becomes the modus operandi for most forgotten conscripts. Over time, they learn to develop relationships with a wide range of peers while simultaneously not becoming attached so saying goodbye and the looming loss of the friendship is not as difficult. These superficial friendships can prevent military-connected adolescents from developing strong connections with peers. However, in the new digital age, maintaining relationships with friends through social media and other technology has reduced some of these problems.

Being stationed overseas can intensify issues with developing friendships. Tyler (2002) states the first year overseas for military-connected adolescents is the most difficult not because of culture shock but due to the loss of friends and difficulties in developing new relationships. The number of times the family relocates, the timing of the move, and the length of time at the duty station, especially during the adolescent years, all impact the forgotten conscript's ability to make friends.

While the mobile, nomadic lifestyle is not ideal, Ender (2005) asserts there are some silver linings in being able to move to new places throughout childhood including an opportunity to be more self-reflective. Military-connected adolescents also get a chance to leave a school that is not conducive to learning and are given a chance to reinvent themselves as they enroll in a new school.

PARENTAL DEPLOYMENT

Parental separation is difficult for all children, but the danger of deploying to a war zone adds an extra layer of stress for forgotten conscripts. Of the four million military-connected children in the U.S., nearly 900,000 have had at least one parent deployed since 2001 (Park, 2011), with 212,000 who deployed twice and 103,000 who deployed three or more times to conflict regions (Chandra et al., 2010). The number of service members deployed from 2001 to 2007 jumped from 8% to 38% and the length of deployments increased from six to 15 months at a time (Engel, Gallagher & Lyle, 2010).

Huebner et al. (2007) states that military-connected adolescents who experience parental separation during identity development are more susceptible to attachment issues, especially if forced to endure multiple deployment cycles. Lester et al. (2010) and Segal (1986) both stress that increased anxiety during parental deployment stems not only from worrying while the parent is away but also from how the family will adjust to the soldier's return.

Separation impacts military-connected adolescents differently than elementary-aged children since teens often take on more responsibility while the soldier parent is gone. Those enduring parental deployment, according to Masten, Best & Garmezy (1990), are at risk for higher levels of anxiety, anger, depression, and rebellious behavior. While boys tend to handle parental deployments better than girls, some forgotten conscripts take advantage of reduced parental governance, which can cause an issue when the soldier parent returns home.

While the fear of losing a parent is debilitating, a soldier's death can impact the military-connected family and adolescents beyond the loss of a parent. Military benefits only last six months beyond death and families are forced to leave military housing, which, in a sense, strips a part of the military-connected adolescent of a layer of their cultural identity. When all a family has known is taken away, that forfeiture only serves to compound the bereavement with the loss of the military parent.

ACADEMIC AND SCHOOL ISSUES

Department of Defense schools are trained to understand and support the needs of military-connected students. Even though according to Kranke (2019), 80% of military-connected children attend public schools, most teachers are not provided professional development or trained to support this invisible minority, which is a failure on the part of the education system.

Another issue is that most of the data on forgotten conscripts often comes from school counselors or administrators alone. This completely ignores the teachers who are the ones that spend much of their time with the students in this invisible population. Caring relationships with peers and adults are important in the life of a military adolescent, especially in the classroom. Well-developed and supportive student-teacher relationships can serve to buffer the stress military-connected adolescents feel.

Harrison and Vannest (2008) remind educators that military-connected children might have gaps in their academic skills and development because of continued mobility and parental deployment. As such, teacher preparation programs and reoccurring professional development needs to foster an awareness of the military-connected child to meet their social, emotional, and learning needs and work to honor the military culture.

There are other issues military-connected adolescents face in public education. Some schools, especially smaller ones, do not have access to resources or the ability to offer a wide range of courses, while Bradshaw et al. (2010) points out others are hesitant to put military-connected adolescents in key positions on athletic teams or in extracurricular groups for fear of them moving away.

In the past, military-connected adolescents were asked to take or repeat classes for high school credit because of divergent schedules or different graduation requirements. The Department of Defense, the Military Child Education Coalition, and the Department of Education worked together to establish the Interstate Compact on Educational Opportunities for Military Children in 2011. This compact was designed to help reduce and facilitate achievement among military-connected students by focusing on issues that arise during enrollment in new schools, including the transfer of records, access to special programs and extracurricular activities, and course requirements to help military-connected adolescents graduate on time.

IDENTITY DEVELOPMENT CONCERNS

The stressors of high mobility, deployment, and academics issues encountered by forgotten conscripts come at the cost of developing a strong sense of self and personal identity. One common issue among military-connected adolescents is prolonged or delayed adolescent maturity. Since adolescent identity development hinges on peer interaction, the time spent trying to cultivate new friendships after each move to a new duty station put them further behind. Likewise, military-connected adolescents given the opportunity to live abroad may adapt elements of their identity to fit into the dominant culture. However, Hoersting and Jenkins (2011) assert that changing too much each time forgotten conscripts move can also lead military-connected adolescents to feel culturally homeless.

By the time a military-connected child is five, Wertsch (1991) claims he or she has already internalized several of the values inherent in the military culture. Yet, as they grow up, many claim the military lifestyle can feel like assimilation as they feel forced to suppress individual identity or beliefs to perpetuate the myth of always being prepared and exemplifying perfection. The inculcation of the mission-first mentality passes from the soldier to the child and can lead to issues with personal identity and even outright rebellion among military-connected adolescents.

Some forgotten conscripts self-identify as biethnic or bicultural, Moore and Barker (2011) state because they have a hard time getting others to recognize the invisible part of their identity. This consistent need to reaffirm their membership within the military culture can cause weariness, Jordan (2002) states, even to the point that military-connected adolescents simply suppress certain parts of their military identity to avoid the conversation.

Even when they are identified as military-connected children, the experiences are not always pleasant. Military-connected adolescents are 1.7 times more likely to be victimized in public school, sometimes by antiwar sentiments or other forms of bullying (Kranke et al., 2019). Or worse, to have that side of their lives completely ignored.

Although the practice has gone out of favor, soldiers used to be held accountable for the actions of their children, facing punishment or loss of rank depending on the offense the child committed. As such, high expectations were set for behavior, academics, and conduct within the home to ensure they always reflect the best version of the military culture. Although a soldier might no longer be reprimanded for their child's indiscretion, those rigid expectations are still the norm for most military families.

It is important to remember that having a cultural identity and feeling as though one belongs is not the same thing. Some might not feel like those all facets of their identity are welcome. While the military is one group, a soldier's identity can still be divided into their branches of service. Many forgotten conscripts often feel compelled to participate in the joking and rivalry they see adults participate in among the branches, a little like representing a neighborhood or a set in a gang.

The military culture is made up of different races, ethnicities, and religions, so conflicts can arise, despite being a part of the larger entity. The prejudice tends to fade when one must rely on another for survival, and while the military is accepting of diversity, Black military-connected adolescents grow up more acutely aware of their differences, which can result in a double dose of marginalism.

Before 1948, Black soldiers served in segregated companies until President Truman signed an executive order reversing this separation. Although the military sought to end segregation years before it was enacted in education, elements of bias concerning race, gender, and sexual orientation exist in today's military, which is easily perceived not just by soldiers but the forgotten conscripts growing up within the culture.

Scarf et al. (2016) points out that having multiple group and cultural memberships can serve as sources of support or protection to help adolescent during major transitions and life events. Perhaps forgotten conscripts appear resilient because the challenges that come from being a part of this culture give them opportunities to develop relationships with several different groups.

Military-connected adolescent identity, according to Litwack and Foster (1981), is shaded by affiliation with the military culture, so feelings of isolation when off base or around civilian peers are common. The first time many military-connected children realize they are different is when they start to attend public school.

This outsider mentality is even more common among forgotten conscripts whose parents are veterans or soldiers in the National Guard and Reserves than those whose parents are on active duty and stationed near a military base. As Kranke et al. (2019) puts it:

> Military-connected adolescents are at a critical juncture developmentally in their lives, and their responses to feelings of differentness can have lasting implications on their transition to adulthood, formation of meaningful social relationships with peers, academic success, and ability to successfully transition to new environments in future instances. (p. 194)

Without the support they need, military-connected adolescents will have a tougher time making it through their teenage years unscathed.

MILITARY-CONNECTED ADOLESCENT STRENGTHS

Despite stressors, military-connected adolescents acquire strengths associated with being a member of this invisible minority. The obstacles for forgotten conscripts are numerous, as they deal with difficulties in building nurturing relationships and developing personal autonomy. However, according to O'Leary and Ickovics (1995), facing these challenges and living to tell the tale can help them develop resiliency to defeat future adversity. They come to cultivate personal strength through passive acceptance that the world is always going to change. This develops into the resilient skill of learning to adapt to any situation.

Socially, military-connected adolescents develop a better sense of well-being, greater respect for authority, and are more likely to befriend someone different from them. Youth within the military culture also tend to fare better, Williamson et al., (2018) states because of the easy access to quality healthcare, at least one steady stream of income for the family, and access to better resources and opportunities.

Blum (2005) reminds us that even though moving so often can hinder them, learning how to meet new people and quickly develop extrovert behaviors can help military-connected adolescents learn to be resilient in both social and work environments. These skills will come in handy as these youth move to new cities, start new jobs, and meet new people.

Soldiers must have a high school diploma or GED to enlist and 25% go on to earn college degrees (Knox & Price, 1999). Military-connected adolescents are four times more likely to attend college than civilian students. The military has been recognized as a viable path for young adults, especially those with high-risk backgrounds, which translates into better opportunities for them and their families according to Masten (2013).

Despite challenges, military families and the military culture give adolescents a meaningful identity associated with strength, service, and sacrifice. Forgotten conscripts develop resiliency and engage in fewer high-risk behaviors than their peers, which, according to Milburn and Lightfoot (2013), often results in lower alcohol or drug dependence issues when compared to civilian counterparts. Easterbrooks et al. (2013), claims military-connected adolescents can develop certain strengths including better self-regulation, academic performance, emotional well-being, and a better community and cultural sense. Moreover, the military is built upon the notion of helping and doing for others, so military-connected adolescents raised in a culture that exemplifies these principles are more likely to internalize them as a part of their own identity.

During time stationed in a different country, forgotten conscripts are more likely to seek out international experiences and travel, allowing them to grow up open-minded. Military-connected adolescents, whether they remain a part of the military as adults, still internalize the idea that they will always be welcomed and accepted by the culture. Perhaps the best strength military-connected adolescents gain from being part of the military is the reliability that membership in this culture endures throughout their lives.

INSIGHT FROM MILITARY-CONNECTED ADOLESCENTS THEMSELVES

Military-connected adolescents are talked about by researchers and educators, but far too often neglected as a wellspring of knowledge. As such, *Forgotten Conscripts* will investigate various experiences military-connected adolescents face and their perceptions on how those events have impacted them during their formative years. Nine military-connected adolescents—Bailey, Brandon, Daisy, Elias, Frank, Leslie, Lindsey, Sage, and Zion—will share their insights and perspectives throughout the remaining chapters of this book. Chapter 2 will focus on identity development among forgotten conscripts and the remaining chapters will feature a spotlight on one or more of these nine military-connected adolescents as the book highlights the experiences, perceptions, and responses to growing up as a forgotten conscript into this invisible minority.

Both similar and divergent, their insight provides revealing and compelling portraits of life within the military culture as it is their voices that will help guide the learning throughout this book. Basic demographics on each of the nine military-connected adolescents are featured in Table 1.1.

Table 1.1. Basic Demographics of Military-Connected Adolescents Featured in the Book

Name	Age	Race	Gender	Grade	Branch of Service	Military-Connected Parent/Guardian
Bailey	18	Caucasian	Female	12	Army	Sister, active duty
Brandon	16	Black	Male—(FtM)	11	Army	Mother, active duty; father, retired
Daisy	17	Caucasian	Female	12	Marines	Father, active duty
Elias	16	Hispanic and Asian	Male	10	Army	Father, active duty
Frank	16	Caucasian	Male	10	Army	Father, active duty
Leslie	18	Caucasian and Black	Female	12	Army and civilian contractor	Father, retired
Lindsey	17	Black	Female	12	Army	Father, active duty
Sage	18	Black	Male	12	Army	Father, active duty
Zion	18	Black	Male	12	Army	Mother, retired; father, retired; stepmom, prior service; stepdad, retired

Chapter 2

The Identity of the Forgotten Conscript

Upon entering military service, soldiers are issued a series of items. A set of battle dress uniforms, a pair of boots, a helmet, and, of course, a weapon. These items offer protection as they work to defend the rest of us.

Sending a soldier into combat without these vital items would be insane.

As forgotten conscripts, military-connected adolescents have limited say in the choices thrust upon them as they grow up. The only control they *do* have is how they respond to the experiences faced within the military culture. As no one issued them anything when they were drafted into this life because they are . . . after all . . . forgotten, most develop identity traits that work as a protective shield. A way to defend themselves from undue harm.

One of the most basic weapons, dating back to the late Stone Age, is the mace. A bludgeoning weapon, similar to a club, maces are simple yet effective in protecting the wielder from adversity. While the use of maces in combat has subsided, they still are symbolic of protection and duty today.

It is this weapon—developed as a part of their identity—that forgotten conscripts use as their own form of protection. By viewing themselves as *mature*, *adaptable*, *confident*, and *empathetic*, it is this MACE that helps military-connected adolescents battle the adversities brought on because of their upbringing within the military culture.

By using the beliefs, experiences, words, and emotions of the nine adolescents presented in the previous chapter, one can see how personal and cultural identity is developed and how military-connected adolescents perceive and define themselves as they develop their MACE identity.

PERSONAL AND CULTURAL IDENTITY DEVELOPMENT

Before diving into the MACE identity developed among military-connected adolescents, it is important to discuss how identity is both personally and culturally cultivated among this age group.

Culture doesn't just surround people, it impacts, it influences, it has the ability to glue groups together (Hylmö, 2002; Moore & Barker, 2011). Teenage years can be tumultuous enough, but forgotten conscripts are additionally impacted by the expectations and experiences of the military culture.

Personal identity refers to the individual goals, values, and beliefs, while *cultural identity* encompasses the extent to which one considers group identification significant and seeks to develop solidarity within it (Schwartz et al., 2012). Specific qualities of individual identity may differ from group to group, but different stages of development often have common elements across cultures.

In 1968, Erik Erikson published his seminal *Identity: Youth and Crisis*. Under the premise of his philosophy, the path from birth to adulthood includes navigating eight distinct stages where identity and crisis converge as both seek to define and impact the person. It is important to note that people should avoid the denotative meaning of the word *crisis* here as adolescent life challenges should be viewed as opportunities and avenues for change as opposed only to adverse events to overcome.

Each stage of development is characterized by a conflict or crisis with the possibility of polar outcomes. Positive results will become the dominant part of the identity if the crisis is worked out, or the negative option will take over if the conflict remains unresolved, which can manifest into adverse mental health and issues with self-concept. Erikson states all eight stages are ever-present—as they exist as a part of the whole person—but individuals must arrive at each stage at the right time to mold a healthy identity.

A military hierarchy that places the needs of its forgotten conscripts behind the mission and the soldier is not always conducive to positive identity development. Military-connected adolescents undergo high mobility, thus have difficulties in establishing strong peer relationships.

Issues with relationships often coincide with late-stage identity development, where adolescents no longer rely on the adults in their lives as role models they seek for guidance and instead place an overwhelming focus on what peers think. Without the development of those healthy peer relationships, forgotten conscripts can become confused about who they are, which can result in rash behavior and self-destructive practices.

Goal development also begins during this stage, where teens leave dreams of becoming superheroes behind to think practically about career and lifestyle aspirations. Fidelity, introduced in the infancy trust stage, makes a reappearance here as a source of strength for teenagers, allowing them to build the autonomy and resiliency to guide them into adulthood. But, like any child that deals with parental abandonment, continual deployments and extended training that takes the soldier parent away for long periods can result in issues with trust that plague teens into adulthood.

Adopting an identity after considerable exploration yields the most success, while personal agency during this development allows for a better understanding of individual identity within a cultural context. Hylmö (2002) points out that perceived membership within subgroups shapes individual experiences and identity differently, so promoting healthy adolescent identity development in conjunction with cultural identity development is crucial.

Molding a stronger cultural identity can help individuals find their place within society, boost self-esteem and sense of belonging, and serve as a protection to overcome oppression and discrimination. As forgotten conscripts consistently move into new cultures and regions of the world, their sense of cultural identity is clearly impacted. This might be why military-connected adolescents develop friendships with fellow military youth as their identity is deeply shaded by their military affiliation.

THE MACE OF THE MILITARY-CONNECTED ADOLESCENT

Learning to protect oneself from harm is one of the first lessons humans learn in life. Be it physical, emotional, or mental health, it is important children develop these skills while they are young so they can continue into adolescence and adulthood.

These four facets of military-connected adolescent identity—maturity, adaptability, confidence, and empathy—work to protect these forgotten conscripts as they experience a world quite different from their civilian counterparts.

Maturity

Developed through guidance and experience, maturity is vital as teens navigate growing up. Military-connected adolescents seem to have to traverse this terrain at a much earlier age than most. However, as they face situations civilians often do not, military-connected adolescents deem their maturity manifests into a higher level of respect, self-reliance, and discipline to help them overcome impediments.

As a core value of the military structure, it is only natural to assume respect would filter down to military-connected adolescents. It becomes a natural thing for them to temper emotions because giving someone "attitude," even if they do not want to do what was being asked of them, is deemed disrespectful.

In fact, most adults claim it "makes sense" when they find out a teen is a forgotten conscript as most associate membership in this culture with being innately respectful. Growing up with military parents, who are expected to show respect as a facet of military protocol, aids them to develop and internalize this behavior as part of their identity. Most claim showing respect to their elders is also a form of pride in themselves.

Continuous deployment and training that takes the military parent from home increase the likelihood of military-connected adolescents learning to do things on their own. Since the person who is supposed to teach them—either implicitly or by setting a positive example—is gone, forgotten conscripts have to figure out how to do many tasks often not required of their civilian counterparts. As such, self-reliance becomes an important trait they develop to survive.

Whether it is mimicking a military parent, avoiding becoming a burden at home, learning to push themselves in school, practicing self-love, or expressing the maturity that comes as people accomplish a goal on their own, self-reliance is a mainstay among this population. While most have their immediate family at home, they consistently express that growing up within the military culture feels like they *are* on their own, so they must learn to trust and rely on themselves from a very young age.

While soldiers are expected to put their life on the line to defend themselves, their fellow brothers- and sisters-in-arms, and the nation back home, self-sacrificing among military-connected adolescents is discounted. Whether it is accepting that the soldier parent will not make their big game or might miss out on their sweet 16th birthday because of their obligation to the military, forgotten conscripts are expected to simply suck it up and accept disappointment. To ensure the family operates smoothly, discipline and delayed gratification go hand in hand.

Acting "wild" like other teenagers is out of the question. Chores are not something they can just "do later." And if born the eldest child, adult responsibilities like getting groceries and driving around younger siblings often fall on their shoulders, especially when the military parent is gone. Yet, despite resenting the expectation to sacrifice when they were younger, many forgotten conscripts admit these demands helped them to develop the maturity they see now as a positive part of their identity.

Adaptable

Change is an issue for some, yet forgotten conscripts learn that being blindsided by it is just a natural rhythm of life for them. Accepting that nothing is promised, life is random, and change is inevitable transforms into a level of adaptability most military-connected adolescents wear like a security blanket.

To make sense of the randomness of their lives, military-connected adolescents perceive themselves as resilient, learn to accept a limited locus of control, and often become masters of unpredictability. It becomes the one constant they know they can always rely on when the rest of the world appears to be spinning out.

Resiliency, the ability to bounce back from a setback, helps military-connected adolescents develop "thicker skin" when facing the inevitable changes that come with military life. This trait is displayed in their ability to circumnavigate each new duty station, new school, or new deployment. It may not become easier, but this change is a constant current in the river of their lives.

Most forgotten conscripts claim their families are stronger than civilian families because while the experiences can be devastating, learning to endure them and come back more resilient than before is a natural byproduct of this lifestyle. One of the best metaphors of this resiliency is to look at military life as a tree that grows for a few years before ripping it out and replanting it in a new place, hoping to nurture it back to grow yet again.

Even though many military-connected adolescents perceive several aspects of this life as a privilege, the fact that they do not have much control throughout their lives weighs heavy on them. Coming of age in the military culture means never being able to plan without the looming fear of change pulling the rug out beneath them leaves these youth feeling less than aplomb.

An extreme byproduct of this limited locus of control is concern about abandonment and trust. Many forgotten conscripts claim the transient life of a military kid leads to a desire to keep others "at arm's length" because having to say goodbye becomes more difficult after each iteration. This, mixed in with the perceived lack of control, can result in a rather lonely life.

Whether they call themselves tough or flexible, military-connected adolescents are adaptable to change at a level far superior to their civilian peers. Dealing with the unpredictability of this life is like building up a callous, tough at first, but eventually, it gets easier. They understand that their parent's job demands far more than others, so they simply find a way to survive.

Some approach it from a place of calm, while others choose to approach adversity head-on. However, forgotten conscripts point out that this level of adaptability does not mean they change who they are at their core. Achieving a balance between adaptation and assimilation is what helps them to master the instability of growing up as a military-connected adolescent.

Confidence

To mask feelings of vulnerability and fear, most adolescents embrace a stance of indifference, as though it will make them impervious to adulthood.

Never has, never will.

Military-connected adolescents are no different, but it is the culture of the military that often forces them to understand childhood is fleeting and they better learn how to navigate this world. Which they do, often with confidence not found among their peers. This confidence is expressed among forgotten conscripts through determination, self-assured fearlessness, a strong sense of personal pride, and optimism for the future.

The military requires soldiers to compartmentalize personal safety for the sake of the mission, so it is only natural this determination is modeled at home. As stated before, at a certain age, peer approval becomes a driving force of identity development, but often it is solely about appearance and not actual substance. It could be said teens are the epitome of the phrase "fake it until you make it."

Yet, among military-connected adolescents, there is a desire to not just look confident, but a determination to be better themselves at every opportunity. The determination to achieve success is what pushes them academically, athletically, and socially. Forgotten conscripts develop an innate leadership ability that pulsates around them.

As they grow up, this confident determination translates into self-assured fearlessness among the youth of this culture. Because the natural rhythm of their formative years beats to the drum of unpredictability, military-connected adolescents learn to trust themselves to find a way through just about anything. They find they fear the notion of the unknown far less than their civilian friends.

It is important to note that each forgotten conscript approaches confidence in their own way. Those imagining a Prince Valiant type might be disappointed. Military-connected adolescents express levels of introversion and extroversion just like any other group, but when mixed with this unwavering lack of fear in the face of the unknown, their confidence results in their own form of leadership that is no less inspiring.

No matter how their confidence manifests and even though they were conscripted into it, forgotten conscripts are proud of their membership within this community. Some express it outwardly with Army shirts, Marine lanyards, and the like. Then some reveal it through their actions, walking with their "heads up, chest out," or the pride that comes from sharing their experiences living across the globe.

This pride often transforms into other areas of activism and gratification like feminism, LGBTQ+ rights, and other areas of activism. The confidence cultivated in one area gives forgotten conscripts the bravery to venture into others and serve as natural leaders.

Most would agree that the life of a military brat is filled with hardships and sacrifice. Yet there is optimism that overshadows the negative experiences for many. Forgotten conscripts tend to focus on the experiences of traveling the world, meeting new people, and learning about new cultures over the tougher parts they endure. This optimism helps them to "make the most of what they got under the circumstances," which is a point of view that speaks to the confidence and maturity of these youth.

The military can open doors for soldiers and provide them the stability that they may not have had growing up, something the children of this culture quickly learn to appreciate. Knowing this makes it easy to see why military families tend to be generational as they dispel the hardships in favor of the realistic view of this culture, making them masters of not just resiliency by thriving.

Empathy

When the world thinks of the military, it is sad to say that empathy is not often the first word that comes to mind. But maybe it should.

For all the gun-slinging and war, the military has the rare chance to glimpse behind the veil of another person's life and truth. They get to travel the world to interact and learn from different cultures. Then, they are given the choice: take what they have learned and imagine how they would feel living in another person's world or discard it as an experience, nothing more, and move on with their life.

Forgotten conscripts are given this same alternative.

Maybe it is their age—their youthful naivete—but they tend to pick the former over the latter. They pick empathy over apathy. This is expressed by their willingness to be self-sacrificing when given the opportunity, their humble and considerate nature, and their inclusive views of the world and the people on it.

While the military provides a stable paycheck with access to quality housing, food, and healthcare, the fine print reminds the families that if "the military calls us tomorrow, we have to go." This reminder firmly stamps the trait of self-sacrificing in the DNA of this culture.

Ask any forgotten conscripts and they can share about the holiday their father missed due to training or the high school graduation their mother could not attend due to deployment. Stories like these become a rite of passage for the youth in this culture.

With the ability to travel the world, one could view the life of a military-connected adolescent through rose-colored glasses. Hardships come with each new move, but a promise of a new experience looms around the corner. It is this very thing that helps them to approach the world with a perceived sense of humbleness toward their upbringing.

Self-absorbed behavior may be the menu du jour for teens these days, but it does not often make an appearance among military-connected adolescents. They may have visited places others could only dream of—Italy, Germany, Hawaii—but the notion of "bragging" about it holds them back from sharing those experiences freely for fear of looking like they are "showing off." Despite being conscripted into this life, most recognize the privilege that also comes with membership and try to learn from each situation—good or bad.

And while social media has allowed them the ease of staying in contact with friends at other duty stations—something not afforded to previous generations of military brats—the desire to make sure they are always Instagram-ready often isn't appealing. No life is perfect, so trying to convince others of the lie is a waste of time, which is a common opinion among forgotten conscripts.

Empathy is only effective if one is a good listener. While most of humanity is capable of hearing, *listening* is an active choice that takes practice. Each time forgotten conscripts move, there is a period of observation, learning the hidden rules of the school and community they have just joined. Listening is a key component of that and something most of these teens pride themselves on doing well, which develops into a reputation of being considerate among their peers. These forgotten conscripts are more likely to join service organizations like Key Club or volunteer at their local church or other charitable organization.

This is not to say that being considerate in all areas is a good thing. Being blinded by the desire to feel less lonely at a new school, most military-connected adolescents admit to making friends with less-than-desirable peers whose reputations were not easily apparent.

Many a military kid has been burned by a friend who took advantage of their kindness and hopes to just fit in as the new kid in school. Or worse, if they developed a negative reputation because of this early friendship, working hard to overcome it is tough as the new kid. In this instance, the transient lifestyle becomes a positive as each new duty station is a chance for forgotten conscripts to reinvent themselves.

Being able to see how others live—here in the U.S. and abroad—exposes forgotten conscripts to the diversity of the world, something many of their civilian peers do not have a chance to partake in. This results in an increased acceptance of others that is not shaded by prejudice or stereotypes others ascribe to. Diversity in the military has a long-standing history and that appears to filter down to the families and children in the military culture.

* * *

It is important to pause here and point out that trying to classify military-connected adolescents under one definition is as futile as it is foolish. While betting on these youth to be mature, adaptable, confident, and empathic would probably place one firmly in the black, it is not a guarantee that each forgotten conscript will develop their MACE to the same extent. Lindsey states it best with her desire for people to know more about military-connected adolescents like her, but with the realization that they are as varied as people in any other culture or group:

> all of [us] are not the same. Some people are a lot more social and outgoing and some of us would not even try. Just indifferent about the whole thing. And then there are those that are like just really shy, they don't like to talk. So, this is just not one prime example of what a military child is. It's multiple variations of us.

Military-connected adolescents may be members of the same culture, but each one is a unique individual and his or her identity goes deeper than any generalization that could be made here. While the MACE is an effective metaphor to showcase the foremost facets of a forgotten conscript's identity, it is not a rigid representation. This is important for educators to remember.

Chapter 3

High Expectations for Forgotten Conscripts

From the outside, Zion, 18, appears to be your typical high school student-athlete. Focused on sports—both playing and watching them—while most of his friends fall firmly in the stereotypical "jock" category. Yet below the surface is something he admits is a significant difference between him and his civilian peers: maturity because of high expectations growing up as a forgotten conscript.

Despite the jealousy that came from this comparison when he was younger, Zion, the son of not one but four military parents, admits the expectations placed on him throughout his childhood were a blessing that helped him to develop a strong work ethic and internal motivation. It wasn't until he was older that he realized the gift these expectations were for him.

While most of his fellow student-athletes only need to balance academics and athletics, this is not the case for Zion. Beyond school and sports, his parents strongly encouraged him to get a job to help learn responsibility. He participates in a local Black youth fraternity, all while maintaining a social life to enjoy his remaining year in high school.

While it used to be that he would work hard to avoid the inevitable punishment that would come if his grades slipped, this has evolved into setting high hopes for himself during adolescence. As such, he works hard to "actually learn" the material, something he doesn't always see in his friends as their parents "don't really care how their kids do in school as long as they're passing."

The desire to make sure he is proficient and everything is done on time and to a certain level is a clear marker of a military-connected adolescent according to Zion. His parents made sure young Zion knew how to how to cook for himself, do his own laundry, and learn proper manners and respect when talking with an adult—"always a 'Yes sir, yes ma'am' when talking with a grown-up"—with the expectation that he would continue to do these tasks *throughout his adolescence. He said these expectations helped him to feel confident when working and talking with doctors and nurses at the hospital where he worked during high school.*

Some of this pressure comes from the lack of high expectations his parents felt they had placed upon them growing up. Both his biological mother and father felt the military gave them the structure to set them up for success, something they wanted to pass along to Zion, he says. However, it was his stepfather's upbringing that hit this message home. Growing up in Detroit was already "a rough spot," but the fact that his stepfather's dad killed himself in the same apartment when he was just six years old profoundly impacted Zion's stepdad. He grew up with his grandmother, who "never totally loved him," Zion claims, so his stepfather learned to set expectations for himself. This example was quite moving for young Zion.

According to Zion, having strict military parents is even harder when his civilian friends do not understand why he must do things at a certain time and in a certain way. For example, he recalls a time when he was out with his friends at a local bowling alley and got a call that he had forgotten to take out the trash. While most teens know that means they need to complete the task when they get home, Zion knew the expectation was that he returns home now or face the consequences. Or, as Zion puts it, "You just got to do what you got to do. You're just going to start problems if you try to get out of it." Compliance without comment is what Zion perceives is expected of him as a forgotten conscript.

* * *

Parents have certain assumptions concerning behavior and choices for their children as they grow up. These often center but are not limited to respect, responsibility, attitude, and academics. While most adolescents agree their parents want the best for them and push them toward positive outcomes, military-connected adolescents, like Zion, often perceive the expectations placed upon them are much higher than many of their civilian peers.

CHILDREN AS SOLDIERS

Procedures and protocols are standard fares for soldiers. Every duty, every action, every job comes with its own set of instructions, or an SOP (Standard Operating Procedure) for anything and everything one might encounter. There is a running joke that the military would issue an SOP for how to properly go to the bathroom if it could. In an environment where individual thinking is restricted, the authoritarian nature of the military career often bleeds over into how military parents run their homes.

The problem is military children did not sign up to be soldiers, yet they are often treated as such by their military parents. As the rigid hierarchy and chain of command in the military gets applied to the structure of the family, this leaves forgotten conscripts feeling like just another young soldier in the eyes of their parents.

Perhaps the least impactful way this is done is with the use of military lingo within the home or family. Like other cultures, the military has its own lexicon rife with phrases and acronyms outsiders would not understand—see the glossary at the end of the book for common military terms and acronyms educators should understand when working with forgotten conscripts.

For example, a new Army soldier coming home from his or her initial training might say something like this: "At BCT, I excelled in BRM and AIT, we learned how to operate a HEMTT while in full MOPP gear. Plus, one time I saw the XO while doing KP at the DFAC and she said I might make a good officer one day, but OCS would mean I would have to change my MOS, and I don't want to leave CONUS for my first duty station." That is a whole lot of alphabet soup to swallow unless one is familiar with the language of the military.

Most forgotten conscripts claim their parents use phrases like "tracking" or "roger" to signify understanding or are told to "double time" when they need to do something faster. For the most part, these phrases become something the whole family commonly uses—an unintended byproduct of living within the military culture. However, on occasion, the military parent can take it too far and, as Sage says, "sometimes I just have no clue what [my dad] is saying" because he forgets Sage is not *actually* in the military, just a forgotten conscript.

The respect inherent with military rank can also be perceived in negative ways among military-connected adolescents. When a high-ranking soldier is around those of a lower rank, there is an expectation of who is supposed to lead and who is supposed to follow.

While that natural hierarchy exists among most parent-child relationships, military parents can take it to the extreme. Leslie says this was obvious the first time her father tried to teach her how to drive a car. As he was teaching her, it was clear that he "[didn't] know where to draw the line between Captain and dad," often taking the tone she only saw him reserve for the soldiers beneath him at work.

While authority is commonplace in most military families, it can sometimes morph into a level of superiority that can feel oppressive. Leslie claims that while her father always took a controlling role in the home, once he earned the rank of staff sergeant, he started to treat his children and spouse the same way she would see him treat his lower-enlisted soldiers. "I feel like that got it into his head where he started to treat us like [them]. He started treating us like we were beneath him and if we didn't listen to him, we were nothing," she asserts.

Because she perceives her dad's need to control everything while demanding the same respect at home as he would from his soldiers, it reinforces the mindset that he is a soldier first and a father second and as the child, she is expected to fall in line. This does not often result in the most open and honest of relationships.

REGIMENTED CHORES AND DUTIES

Zion is not the only military-connected adolescent to claim that expectations concerning chores and behavior in the home felt more stringent when compared with civilian friends. Daisy insists her friends often point out how "strict" her family is because she cannot come and go as she pleases despite being just a few months shy of 18.

Elias, on the other hand, claims that even dinner in his home comes with its own set of demands, often resulting in an hour-long affair where everyone shares their day until they are dismissed by their father. Elias chuckled in recalling this because he remembers once telling a friend that he had to go to dinner and the friend, who expected him to come back quickly to continue playing a video game, was surprised when he didn't hear back from him until hours later.

While chores in the home are a common way to instill responsibility in any child, the expectations for the depth of those duties are perceived to be sterner in a military home. Gone may be the days where parents would bounce quarters off beds to ensure that they were made nice and tight, but Leslie claims she had to wake up early every Sunday to deep clean the house, often going as far as cleaning baseboards with toothbrushes. "I think this is where my OCD behavior comes from—a life full of Sundays making sure the house was spotless from top to bottom," she asserts.

Elias also endures high expectations for cleanliness in the home, but it was because his mother demands it, pushing his military father in the "drill sergeant role" to ensure the home is cleaned to mom's specific expectations. In this instance, it is the culture that the home parent learned to raise his or her children that were prevalent.

Duties outside the home are often held to the same standard for forgotten conscripts. Bailey, who spent the first decade of her life living with her mother until she opted to move in with her military sister, was able to acutely see this difference, especially in terms of academics. When she was living with her mother, she went to school, but that was it—she just *went*. There was no parental push to do anything beyond simply show up each day.

Her sister, on the other hand, insisted that Bailey not only attend but expected her to do better each day. Bailey claims her sister never seemed satisfied with her progress and achievements, that she was always "fussing at her" and telling Bailey she could do better. "My grades are better than they ever were" because of her sister, Bailey states, as she is finishing up her last year of high school with a solid GPA.

Both Sage and Elias echo those same sentiments. In terms of academics, Sage claims he would only get a reprieve from his dad if it was a "really, really intense class," but if he got a grade lower than a B in any class, his parents would question him about it until the grade improved.

Interestingly enough, Elias claims that it was his civilian mother and not his military father that was the authoritarian when it came from academics for him and his younger brother. "It's just weird," Elias asserts, because growing up he used to be scared of his dad, not his mom, however with academics, dad was happy if the boys did their best, while with mom, "we could always do better," he reveals.

ALWAYS A SOLDIER FIRST

Every job comes with certain expectations and responsibilities but being a soldier in the U.S. Armed Forces is not a traditional 9-to-5 job. Few jobs ask as much of their employees including specific levels of physical fitness, extended time away from family, a willingness to give your life for the sake of the job, and loyalty to the nation above all others. While every soldier recognizes these as a given, it is something forgotten conscripts come to realize as they grow up. In an ordered list of priorities within the family, military-connected children rarely snag that first-place trophy.

While deployment to a war zone will mean time away from home, many forgotten conscripts already deal with the military imposing long workdays on their parents, giving them limited opportunities to see one another. Sage, whose dad works with basic trainees—brand new soldiers going through BCT, their first rounds of military training—sees these long hours as a major constant in his life. As a result, Sage and his twin brother often go entire days without seeing their father beyond his multiple deployments throughout their childhood.

Soldiers also work rotating shifts, even pulling 24-hour duty as directed. This results in the expectation that the children, especially the older ones, will pitch in and take on some of the missing parental responsibility in the home.

While Sage claims to have learned to accept this expectation, Lindsey grew to resent it as she reached her teen years. As the oldest child, she is often expected to start dinner, do the laundry, and take care of her younger sisters, all without complaint. One time she did try to broach the subject with her parents, her military father characterized her reaction as a "little meltdown," so she decided to quit trying to bring it up and just accept these expectations until she graduates from high school.

In terms of attitude and decorum, military expectations for the soldier often trickle down to the military family. Daisy, whose father is a high-ranking officer, would see this each time her father hosted lieutenants graduating from OCS in their home. "There's definitely a pressure to support the military in general and to make sure we're not doing what we're not supposed to be doing. Like making sure that we're always in line," she asserts. This involved hours of house-cleaning, formal attire, and often a desire to be seen and not heard by the new lieutenants, so that the entire family is presenting themselves in a way that "reflect well on [our dad] and the Marine Corps."

This pressure to appear perfect in all situations is something Elias can also relate to. His soldier father, who grew up as a military-connected child himself, instilled in him how the military soldier is often judged by the way his or her family behaves, so there is an expectation to be a "good family" and reflect that back to the military, Elias claims. It felt like if they let down their parent with bad behavior, they were also letting down the military, which is a tremendous amount of pressure for anyone, let alone an adolescent.

This same expectation of behavior is also anticipated when the soldier parent leaves for extended training or another tour of duty. Frank spoke about a time when his father was deployed and word was received that he had been awarded a Bronze Star, a medal given for heroic or meritorious service in a combat zone. It took days for his father to call home with news about what had happened, which felt like torture as they expected the worst.

Frank claims he and his family were expected to remain calm and patient until they received that call, which left him with his wheels spinning, worrying for nearly a week if his dad was even going to come home after doing "something crazy like his job asks him to."

INTERNALIZING HIGH EXPECTATIONS

When someone grows up in an environment where expectations from those in positions of authority are high, it is only natural to assume they will begin to internalize those same guiding principles. Since they already express perceptions of determination, discipline, self-reliance, and adaptability as part of their identity, realizing that forgotten conscripts will adopt high expectations for themselves is easy to imagine.

From a very young age, Sage says he feels he is "advanced over the kids his age" because of the high expectations he learned to develop for himself. He attributes this trait to what helps him remain focused on the future because "in the next few years you're going to be on your own, so it's down to planning since the four most critical years of your life go by really fast," he says.

Seeing the value in school and the importance of being future-oriented is advice Sage wishes he could share with others who might not have been able to internalize the high expectations he feels he has developed as a military-connected adolescent.

Daisy claims that she developed such high expectations for herself that her overachieving desires often meant she would find herself overextended. It was Daisy's experience that she had to take a realistic look at what she could do to make sure that she was successful at a few things instead of simply being mediocre at many.

This advice also relates to Elias and Frank, both sophomores as they start making plans for their future early. Elias plans to take additional core classes to help him prepare to major in engineering in anticipation of applying for a military academy. Frank feels his adopted high expectations helped him as he transitioned from homeschooling to public school the year before high school, which could have felt like a setback without the adaptability he learned from the development of his MACE identity while growing up in the military culture.

Frank claims that to achieve these high expectations and excel in school, he must strive to study more at home and ask his parents and teachers for help when he is not able to understand something or find the answer on his own. Since these expectations are goals he set for himself, had he not developed the internal motivation to achieve them, it would have been easy to despair.

Chapter 4

The Burdens of Being the New Kid

For Frank and Lindsey, a big area impacted by being a forgotten conscript was their education. Each new duty station came with a new school setting to traverse, and they will admit being the new kid every few years is hard.

Frank, 16, attended elementary public school, but before age 10, he began homeschooling with his mom. While there was a DoD school available in Germany where they moved a few years later, the family decided to continue homeschooling with a group of six or seven fellow military-connected adolescents stationed together on base. This continued until the family moved back stateside just before his freshman year of high school.

Frank was "super worried" about his classes when he first moved back to the U.S. and started public school then. He found himself far advanced in English and history but struggling to keep up in his math classes. While he ended up doing well, this was an extra layer of stress placed on the forgotten conscript's shoulders as the family navigated a new duty station.

A lack of understanding that, because of the life they lead, military-connected adolescents might have valuable insight into the global world is also problematic, according to Frank. Since respect is ingrained as a part of his identity, He feels that "it's not your place" to contradict a teacher, but he felt that many were "blind to the fact that some kids have been through more than others," especially military kids like himself. In history class, his desire to share experiences living overseas was often met with an unreceptive demeanor from his teachers, so after a while, he just stopped trying to share at all.

Lindsey, 17, who moved to five different duty stations throughout her youth, states at each new school she "shuts down for a minute" to "regroup" and better understand the school's structure. As an honor student, the lack of AP or honors classes at some schools made it difficult for her to continue to challenge herself with higher-level courses. This resulted in a transcript filled *with courses and electives she did not need—sadly a commonality among many forgotten conscripts.*

Another area impacted is the ability to make friends each time orders are cut and they are forced to pack up their life. The desire to fit in is common for any youth, but for military-connected adolescents, the loneliness can lead some to take the first friend that puts in an application. Lindsey experienced this during a move before high school where she claims to have "lost herself by acting wilder than she normally would have" to make friends. She realizes now that forgotten conscripts need a minute to adjust not just academically but socially, so taking the time to find good friends is healthier than taking whoever is available because you feel alone.

Without the long history made as children growing up together, even now Lindsey struggles to shed her outsider status and find ways to relate to her civilian friends. This is why many forgotten conscripts stress how invaluable it is when fellow forgotten conscripts find one another in a school. Not only does it help to have someone who uniquely understands the demands placed on military brats, but sometimes they get to cross paths again, like Lindsey, whose last duty station was one of the places she previously lived as a child, allowing her to reunite with old friends and thus "making the transition easier."

* * *

Teen years are challenging as adolescents work to figure out who they are and where they fit in the world. Moving every couple of years exacerbates this challenge for forgotten conscripts. While the military has support programs in place, this period of adjustment for students like Frank and Lindsey is just another thing forgotten conscripts experience as a part of this culture.

In some cases, military-connected adolescents moved into a district that is both academically and socially the same or even better, but that is not true each time. No matter where they ultimately attend, each school has an obligation to make new students feel welcome, and that is not just the civilian ones. This is a mantle each school must take up to help forgotten conscripts feel in step with the rest of the students in the school.

ACADEMIC CURRICULUM AND SCHOOL STRUCTURE

Each school a military-connected adolescent enrolls in is not guaranteed to be at the same academic level as the previous one. Be it a change in curriculum paths, an abundance or lack of electives, or moving from a high-tech school to a techno-desert, these changes will place forgotten conscripts ahead of or behind their peers at each new school. In some instances, they can even be both. This is where their adaptive skills as part of their MACE identity come in handy.

Before 2008, state and school districts did not have a consistent policy to help forgotten conscripts meet graduation requirements and determine eligibility for athletics, college, and scholarships. This is where the Interstate Compact comes into play to help forgotten conscripts not fall through the cracks to achieve success and graduate on time.

While the Interstate Compact on Educational Opportunities for Military Children should help forgotten conscripts transition easier into a new school, the keyword is *should*. For it to be effective, it must be well publicized and explained to district officials and parents. Yet, as a compact and not a contract, it is not legally binding, meaning states can choose to enforce it at the levels they deem fit. As such, forgotten conscripts still face extra obstacles to graduate on time.

While Brandon has been at his current school for nearly two years, he still feels like he is having to catch up to where his peers are even after so much time has passed. Frank illustrates this change in two different ways: one, when he moved from Hawaii to Virginia, where he said he went from an extremely low performing school to a top tier one, which "destroyed my early years of school," and two, his experiences in dealing with issues because of his vision and dyslexia, which makes it even harder for him to adjust after each move.

This is something Daisy understands as she would watch her parents struggle to find a school that would be the best fit for her younger brother with Down Syndrome. It is not just about ensuring the school can meet the needs of a child with his disability, but also about finding an accepting and inclusive school for children with exceptionalities. These concerns add extra stress to her family each time they move.

For Daisy, it meant she and her other siblings would selflessly try and figure out how to adapt to a new school on their own so their parents could make her brother's needs a priority. This is another way in which the self-sacrificing facet of her MACE identity bleeds through.

Sage also notices he is at a different level than his peers, although it is not just about the coursework. One of the schools he and his twin brother attended during his first two years of high school felt "more financially stable" as the college-preparatory structure of the school was built under the assumption that they "intended for everyone to go to college." However, when he moved to his current school, there was a dual focus on career paths in addition to college. Although this current school offered different options, he did feel like he missed out on the opportunities he would have had if he were able to complete his high school years at his previous school.

While forgotten conscripts experience different academic rigor and requirements, another experience many encounter is learning to navigate the new school's procedures. Some have different ways of going about basic things like hall passes, off-campus lunch, or homeroom that military-connected adolescents must ascertain to be successful. Additionally, finding out what each teacher expects and how they run their classes was something that becomes part of the checklist they must complete at each new school.

This is not to say that every move is a negative experience for forgotten conscripts. Bailey and Leslie both moved from large high schools to their much smaller current ones, which both claim to be a positive change. At her previous school, "What is your name?" was a consistent question Bailey heard when she talked with the school leadership, but since her current school is just over 200 students in her graduating class, it allows Bailey to be recognized in the hallway by teachers and peers. For Leslie, the move was to a more welcoming school where the teachers work harder to develop "emotional connections with their students." It is her opinion that this helped her to improve socially and academically in her current school environment.

OVERCOMING THE OUTSIDER LABEL

A new person in any situation can feel like a spotlight is being shined upon them. Adolescents, who often already feel as though they and all their perceived imperfections are on display, often have a harder time overcoming these outcast feelings. When you add in the fact that this experience is routinely encountered by forgotten conscripts throughout their childhood, the stress that comes with feeling like an outsider is even more pronounced.

Elias claims he often feels "out of place" among his peers, especially the civilian ones. For Leslie, her feelings of being an outsider were intensified when she moved before high school and tried to make friends. The lack of shared experiences from childhood with her peers made her feel like "the outcast" in most social settings.

Lindsey said one experience stood out to her when she moved the summer before middle school. She made a neighborhood friend over the summer but learned her connection was not as deep as the ones this friend had developed with other peers over the years—something that became abundantly clear when the school year started. While she eventually found her spot among the group, the pain of not being seen as the "best friend" to the neighborhood girl did not hurt any less at the time.

Bailey and Daisy both used the word "stressful" when discussing their experiences with integrating into a new school and finding "good" friends. Elias insists the process of finding new friends is "nerve-wracking" because it feels like being interviewed each time. Most agree these feelings eventually subside and the adaptive nature of being a forgotten conscript makes this experience easier, but the fear of having to go through it again and in the future is always lingering.

A common truth forgotten conscripts learn fast is that good friends do not come with signs. Sometimes the first person lining up to befriend the new kid might be a bad apple instead of a good one. That person might be looking for friends because all their previous relationships went up in a blaze of glory at their own hands. Therefore, many forgotten conscripts have the experience of making a bad decision in the friendship department following a move.

As mentioned previously, Lindsey remembers changing part of her personality to fit in with a popular crowd at school. While the attention was blissful at the time, she knew it was wrong to pretend to be someone she was not. She told herself, "You're not going to just let yourself feel like that again or stoop that low . . . be something you're not," just to make friends and vowed to never lose herself again.

Getting in with the "wrong crowd" was something Daisy did not realize at first until she witnessed some new friends not being nice to classmates, thus casting her in the role as a "mean girl" by proxy in the school. Making the break from these new friends in middle school was hard as she did not have a strong bond with anyone else, so it was like starting all over again. The worst part though was the reputation that followed her because of her earlier mistakes. Even after she realized it and dumped them, she still had to live with the reputation that befriending them initially brought her until they moved again.

HURDLES FOR MILITARY-CONNECTED ADOLESCENT ATHLETES

While academic changes are the way most forgotten conscripts experience difficulties, military-connected adolescents who are also student-athletes encounter additional problems as a result of moving so often.

Bailey, who played volleyball through high school, had some issues with the time frame in which sports seasons are set in different states. Since sports seasons can begin at different times of the year, Bailey had to forfeit an entire season of volleyball her junior year due to moving as a military-connected adolescent. This equated to less time to practice her skills, and less time to create a film for college coaches to see for recruiting purposes.

Sage also has had trouble in sports, but his trouble was in trying to make sure that he was able to be recognized for his ability by the coaches. He felt that as a military-connected student-athlete, he consistently had to "show out" at practice "because [coaches are] not going to easily think, 'Oh because you're new, you're going to be someone as good.'"

Sage admits he knows civilian students move all the time, but often the reputation and name recognition are there as most move within the same district or region of the state. Military-connected student-athletes come from across the globe, so that recognition does not pack up easily in their suitcases.

Since athletics is an avenue where students often display desirable skills beyond academics to attend college and earn a scholarship, military-connected adolescents feel that moving so often is not always advantageous for them athletically and yet another way they must learn to adapt.

Zion felt he was lucky enough to be at the same school for his four years of high school, which allowed him to feel as though he was a part of something bigger than just the student body. However, when new military-connected students would move into the district, he could see how hard it must have been for them to get recognized over the veteran players, so he would often reach out, work with them, and welcome them to the team and the school. Athletics is where he made some of his strongest friendships with fellow forgotten conscripts.

During his senior year, Sage claims he was finally able to experience working with a coach who knew his strengths and weakness as a part of the track team. Since he was there during his junior year, the coaches already had a chance to observe him and were able to help him address areas of concern, allowing him to find greater success in the sport. This experience, though fleeting, was something he wished he had had throughout his high school years as Zion was able to do.

FRIENDSHIPS AMONG MILITARY-CONNECTED ADOLESCENTS

Although it is not a prerequisite, most forgotten conscripts agree that some of their closest friends also happen to be fellow military brats. As mentioned in chapter 1, Wetrsch (1991) referred to it as a "military brat antenna," where military-connected children, who are not even aware of if or how they are doing it, can suss out other forgotten conscripts around them.

Daisy and Leslie both state it is great to have friends who understand the discipline and high expectations that come from living in a military family. This also helps to circumnavigate those awkward conversations of having to explain how priorities and expectations work in a military family.

Frank claims while he never implicitly tries to seek out military-connected adolescents as friends, he believes he might subconsciously do this when he finds himself in a new group of people because then "we have at least one thing in common." The experience of creating a bond with fellow forgotten conscripts overseas happens much faster and even goes deeper, he claims, because it feels like "it was you against the world" when stationed in a different country.

According to Sage, "other military kids understand the situations you go through" that civilian friends simply cannot. Not having to explain why your family has specific expectations or why you might keep people at arm's length is an advantage many perceive in looking to find relationships among those living within the military culture. Being able to have close friends who do not just empathize but personally understand the hardships of growing up in this culture is invaluable.

Another positive aspect of developing friendships with fellow military-connected adolescents is the fact that you might be able to see them if you cross paths again when new orders to move are given to the family. Although people do change—something that Leslie and Lindsey both found out when they moved to a previous post after being gone for a few years—the likelihood of falling back into an old friendship alleviates some of that stress of being the new kid yet again.

Since high mobility is a given within the military, these youth admit that one of the hardest things about the move is saying farewell to the friends they have made. One thing that has made it easier to maintain friendships after moving is remaining connected through technology.

According to Brandon, it must have been harder for previous generations who only could rely on letters mailed across states or long-distance phone calls to keep up with friends after a military move. But with social media, the friends Brandon made with people in Kentucky or Georgia are still as strong as they were when he lived there, he asserts.

Elias points out that while this is a plus when you are a teenager, trying to stay connected to those you met when you are much younger is harder. This is not just about access to technology, "but as you grow up, you grow apart as well," so without the proximity, the friendship often dies away.

Daisy explains she experienced some issues with anxiety and even jealousy concerning how difficult it was going to be to continue friendships via distance. The worry about the friend moving on or "forgetting about me," is hard, so social media has made the immediacy of the friendship easier, thus making it better to keep the fire of friendship lit across state or national boundaries.

While most will agree that being the new person in school is tough for any adolescent, forgotten conscripts face barriers academically and socially that make the process more arduous, thus the need for schools to learn how to recognize those obstacles and work to alleviate them as much as possible.

Chapter 5

Deployment and Reunification of the Military Family

Thirteen was an important year for Leslie. It was the last time her dad deployed and the age just before she moved to her family's final duty station. Thirteen is also the year, according to her, that she feels like she really lost her dad. "I would say 13 was a pivotal year for me." Saying farewell to a loved one is arguably hard on everyone. But, like a revolving door, military-connected children encounter this experience again and again and again.

Leslie, who likens herself to a "tumbleweed blown across the globe," claims deployment is the most taxing part of being a military brat. The youngest of two kids—and a surprise to boot as doctors told her mother she would never be able to have another child after their son was born—young Leslie felt comfortable within the military culture. She loved seeing new places and meeting new people every few years. However, when her father would have to go away for training, she took it the hardest in the family.

This is not to say that she felt completely abandoned. Leslie credits her mom, who would put her own feelings of fear aside to help ensure her children felt supported and loved during these difficult times away from their father. "As I've gotten older, I started appreciating her more because of the things that I realized she was doing and had been doing for us all along," she states.

Leslie's dad deployed to Afghanistan when she was in middle school and while the many months apart and lack of reliable communication was arduous, the hardest part, she found, was yet to come. "He came home . . . different." Her once happy-go-lucky father was now moody, angry, and sought to detach himself—both physically and emotionally—from his wife and children. This resulted in anxiety and depression that debilitate Leslie and her mom to this day.

Leslie's relationship with her father was once again affected during her final years of high school. A year after his retirement, her father decided to leave the family and become a government contractor working overseas, this time throughout her entire senior year. This is a common route many retired military soldiers take as they have a large skill set that doesn't always translate to a civilian career.

At the end of that year apart, her father dropped a big bombshell on the family: he met someone else while working abroad and planned to divorce Leslie's mom and marry this other woman. He essentially decided he wanted a do-over, only with a whole new family, which only compounded Leslie's issues with trust and feelings of rejection.

Leslie understands that what her dad witnessed and survived during his deployment changed the fabric of who he was to who he is now, and while she does not blame him for this change—after all, "he was just following orders"—she admits she has a hard time not blaming the military for what she views as the loss of her father in her life.

* * *

A soldier knows they must be prepared to enter combat at any time—it is why they spend so much time training, to be prepared for anything. Yet the military family and forgotten conscripts must be prepared as well. Prepared to say goodbye, prepared to move, prepared to give up their parent for the safety and security of the nation.

Since the World Trade Center attacks in 2001, this generation has witnessed a nation engaged in continuous rounds of military actions and deployments to war zones. It is almost as though these forgotten conscripts are prepared for anything . . . except for peace. There are many experiences that military-connected adolescents endure and adapt to during deployment and reunification once the soldier parent returns home.

CHANGES IN THE HOUSEHOLD

When an adult in the home heads off to military training, deployment, or an unaccompanied tour of duty, the responsibilities in the home do not travel with them. And while the children cannot fill the shoes of the absent parent, many forgotten conscripts claim they experienced an increase in the amount and type of duties around the home that were expected of them. This was even more prevalent if one is unlucky enough to be born an older child in the home.

For Bailey, the hardest part about her older sister and guardian's deployment is how the routines in the house have been disturbed. The first deployment she was gone, Bailey claims she got used to it—and to being apart—but since her stay with her sister has become a permanent thing, "it is hard because like I woke up every day and saw her and now I don't." Bailey states that because this deployment was during her final months of high school, all the senior year things—finals, scholarships, college applications, prom, and graduation—became her sole responsibility and it was challenging to make these decisions on her own.

Although not a physical task, Elias stated he experienced the pressure to be a "father figure" for his younger brother in his dad's deployment. He believed it was important to him to step up and do more to help, but he felt out of his depth much of the time. Understandable when one remembers he was only a teenager.

Frank explained he had a similar experience, but his focus was on stepping up to help his mom and make sure the home runs smoothly for them, his younger siblings, and the two foster children the family has taken in to care for as well.

One of the worst things was when they would all go out in public and he stated he could feel the stares of people who "automatically assumed she was a single mom raising all these kids," so he would often wear an Army shirt whenever they would go out during his father's deployment or training so it would "kind of like subconsciously tell everybody, you know, our dad is in our life."

The increase of stress on the home parent is something most forgotten conscripts watched occur during deployment or extended tours of duty. Both Sage and Elias point out how grateful they were for the sacrifices their home parent made to take on the needs of the family. Lindsey states that she did not understand how much the deployment impacted her mom until she was older. "I think it put a lot of pressure on my mom when my dad was away, just to make sure me and my sisters were good." Upon reflection, she wishes her mother would have shared more of her feelings as it could have been an opportunity for them to bond more.

She also found out later that her parents were also going through some marital issues while her dad was deployed the last time, which Lindsey states, "had to have been really tough on her because deployment is hard enough without adding on more stress." Lindsey claims her mom never openly showed her struggle to her and her sisters, but in retrospect, it makes sense why they would "go visit grandparents so often so they could help take the load off of our mom."

The stress Leslie claims her mom experienced because of her father's deployment was "debilitating enough to cause her to suffer from severe depression." In a similar way that Lindsey's parents suffered some marital strife due to deployment, Leslie's parents' struggles were only intensified when her dad was deployed to Afghanistan. Her mother's depression during her father's deployment was so incapacitating, Leslie states her older brother's girlfriend moved in with the family to help where her mother simply could not.

Keeping in contact with their military parent while they were deployed has never been an easy thing. While the days of having to wait weeks or months for a reply are residuals of the past, this is still an area with issues. Granted, technology has made it easier from the letter-only days of the past, but as Murphey's Law dictates, anything that can go wrong often does.

Some remember writing letters or sending care packages filled with pictures, favorite foods, and other sentiments of home while others received telephone and video calls. However, many spoke about experiencing those sparingly and that they were often unreliable means of communication.

For Zion, his parents deployed when he was very young, but he remembers writing letters and drawing pictures to mail. Lindsey also remembers sending and receiving care packages, especially during Christmas when her dad was deployed. With such a large family, Daisy's family was featured in a CNN News segment about Valentine's Day during deployment. Daisy, who was four or five at the time, remembers having to open a "fake" letter from her dad while they filmed it, which she insists was a surreal experience.

One thing military-connected children can agree on was the unreliable nature of communication with the military parent. Frank remembers being able to Skype dad "like every day" while he was stationed in Korea, which he had assumed he would still be able to when he was deployed to Afghanistan and was devastated when they would go weeks without contact.

Leslie remembers that sometimes the lighting would be so bad on the video call that "all you could see is like his teeth," while Elias laughs when thinking back on those phone calls as half of the time, one or both parties would utter the phrase, "Can you hear me now?" Yet, Elias admits that even though technology concerns made it difficult, he still thinks the experience of being able to talk with his dad in some capacity was always better than reading and writing letters.

While most forgotten conscripts can remain with their home parent while their military parent was sent to a conflict zone, this was not always possible. Some experience living in a different environment while their loved ones are gone for a trip downrange or some other military training.

Brandon remembers having to stay with a grandmother during long training periods that his parents would have as a dual military family, but he was very little at the time, so the impact was minimal he claims. While he and his younger brother lived mostly with his mother after his parent's divorce, he remembers having to move to stay with his dad, who had retired from the military, during one of his mom's deployments.

Bailey had to live with her sister's new wife for the remaining months of her senior year when her sister deployed to the United Arab Emirates. However, this was not the first time that she had to live with someone else while her sister was gone for something related to her military career. "Before we moved here, she was married, but they got a divorce. When she went to Kentucky to train, I stayed with the ex for a few months and, yeah, it was weird." After the move to live with her sister became permanent, whenever long-term training would come up, Bailey would stay at a friend's house during those weeks. While time apart is the hardest, Bailey said that having to adjust to a new living arrangement each time her sister went somewhere was a close second.

No one in this book experienced a harder living arrangement during deployment than Sage. While he and his twin brother stayed with mom during one of his dad's deployments, Sage knew she would not be in a place—emotionally and financially—to take care of them when his dad got orders to deploy when they were in the 7th grade. The next best guardian for the brothers at the time was not even technically a family relative anymore. Dad had just divorced his second wife in Colorado and the woman who ended up taking them in was actually "my dad's ex-wife's sister, so technically, she was my ex-stepmom's sister." Not an ideal situation.

The boys had to pack up and leave Colorado behind to live with this "aunt" in Virginia for the year. This was hard enough but, "she already has a lot of kids to take care of," so he and his brother feel both ignored and like they were an imposition. Sage states he was grateful for what this woman did for his family, but he perceives this as a tough experience because it was not only hard to be without his father—and a mother as well—but to feel like you are an outsider in the home that you are living in at the time made an already hard situation even more heartbreaking.

FEELINGS OF ABANDONMENT

While many forgotten conscripts see the heightened stress for the home parent, they also see how having to grow up without one or both of their parents for an extended period impacted them in many ways.

Any deployment is an emotional event, according to Zion, who claims that the experience of his parent's deployment was even harder than dealing with their divorce during his childhood. Sage says he was always a bundle of different emotions whenever his father was gone. He would go through the emotions of being sad and scared, but "there's no way to describe it. Sometimes I would not think about it at all because he has already been through a couple of times and came back fine." He says the constant worry about whether his dad was going to come home was sometimes so much he would have to try and do other things to keep himself occupied so he wouldn't think about it.

While Frank states all forgotten conscripts go through "a season where it'll be bad or stressful or you know sad because your dad's gone," Lindsey claims that each person deals with deployment differently in her experience. For her, she said she was happy that her parents did not try to "paint a rosy picture" and opted instead to be honest with her and her sisters during her dad's deployments. She adds it made it easier for her to deal with the feelings of abandonment because ultimately, she knew where he was and why he was there.

However, because she was aware of where her father was, the constant barrage of media coverage made it worse for Lindsey and her other friends who were also military-connected adolescents. She saw this impact her most academically. She claims that when he deployed for the second time in 2009, she would come home and "watch the news, sobbing . . . which wasn't a good thing for a seven-year-old to be doing."

Lindsey also remembers a parent of a child in her school who died overseas during her dad's deployment and when she learned about that, her worried nature only intensified. She stated all of this put her in an emotional space where she would freak out and overreact, which resulted in her earning low marks for all her classes until her father finally returned home safely from deployment later that year.

On the other hand, both Brandon and Elias express different sentiments regarding the impact of deployment and parental absences. For Brandon, he does not remember his mom being gone really "fazing him in a negative way" because he claims he just learned to adapt to his parents moving in and out of his life due to their career. Elias claims that because his dad was gone so often during his youth, he began to feel desensitized to the experience to the point that "it doesn't affect [him] anymore."

Most forgotten conscripts believe age makes a difference on the level of impact the deployment has on them. Zion, who watched his parents deploy when he was very little, says he believes it would have been much harder had he been older. "Middle school is like, when you're in that transition and you kind of need your parents to guide you, you know, to your high school life," he states.

Frank agrees with Zion's reasoning completely and claims that even though his dad deployed multiple times throughout his life, the deployment during his freshman year of school was his "toughest one so far." Elias explains that the reason why deployment is harder when you are older ties back to the concept of ignorance being bliss. "I was really young at the time, so I never really understood what it meant and then, because I was older, I had to kind of understand what was going to happen and everything," he asserts. Because he was a child who had a limited grasp on what was happening, Elias added that it was easier to be distracted from what was happening—or *could* happen—to his father during deployment.

Lindsey, who experienced deployment both as a child and an adolescent insists it was harder for her when she was older, but also sees how it could be tough when you are younger because of the way it impacted her little sister.

She states her elementary-aged sister would become distraught when they could not "just call their dad or talk with him for longer." Each phone call would end in tears as her sister would "act out" each time they would hear from their dad. They would have to try to explain it to her again because, at her age, she simply could not understand the situation. While deployment is unpleasant at any age, these military-connected adolescents feel that experiencing it when one is younger results in less of an impact on forgotten conscripts.

HAPPY HOMECOMING

Welcoming home a loved one from war is a joyous and emotional experience for forgotten conscripts. However, helping the soldier parent transition back to normal life comes with its own set of trials and tribulations.

Ask any forgotten conscripts and they will remember the experience of welcoming home their mom or dad from deployment as a festive occasion. Often these ceremonies are a big deal, filled with music and balloons, signs and streamers, and all the pomp and circumstance befitting the event. But for the children, it is the anticipation of, as Zion put it, "finally being able to hug them." The experience was so impactful for him that whenever he views military homecoming videos, he still "tear[s] up a little."

Sometimes the experience is made even better when the homecoming is a surprise for members of the family. Leslie says that when her dad came back when she was younger, they were able to surprise her brother when they picked him up from school that day because they did not tell him that dad had come home early.

The return of Lindsey's father in elementary school was supposed to be a surprise, but she said that her teacher misread the email and accidentally told the secret to Lindsey in school one day. She claims she was just as elated even though the surprise was ruined.

However, for Daisy, her father was able to surprise her at school when he returned by setting it up with her computer teacher to come in and see her for the first time in months. "I was so shocked because he came up behind me and said 'Surprise,' and I knew it was his voice. I just started crying I was so happy," she claims. She knew that her father was going to be coming home soon since they had made a big sign to put up on the house but making it a surprise for her made it even better for Daisy to reunite with her dad.

Frank also remembers making signs to welcome back his dad from deployment, but he says he never experienced the big homecoming ceremony "like, you know, you see on TV." Since his dad never deployed in a group of larger than 15–20 people, the welcome home ceremonies were much smaller, which is standard procedure for the military. Although it was small, Frank claims that it did not diminish the level of emotion that came from being able to hug his dad for the first time in months.

The level of emotion that comes with a military homecoming was something that Elias states he did not quite understand until it happened:

> you think that it's just going to be a good simple hug and let's get out of here but that what ends up happening is you start going through the emotions. It is all of a sudden . . . just, I don't know, where you start breaking into tears, hugging him. I remember the first time I saw my dad. I didn't even remember. I didn't recognize him, [he] changed so much and I hugged him. When I hugged him, I just broke down and it was funny because my dad was like telling me, "It's okay son. It's okay."

Elias, who admits that he is reluctant to show emotion in most situations, was surprised by how quickly and overwhelming they rose to the surface when he was finally able to welcome his dad back after his deployment.

NOT ALWAYS EASY TO COME HOME

While feelings of euphoria are common at the beginning, those can fade when the military parent begins to reintegrate into the family. Elias asserts that some of these problems were because "the fears in the soldier's eyes is when they get deployed, they're going to be out of the loop." While the military parent was gone, life continues for the rest of the family, and forgotten conscripts, such as Elias, continue to grow up, which can make the soldier parent feel like they were "frozen in time" when they return home.

Forgotten conscripts claim reintegration is often a tricky experience for several reasons. Sometimes, the military parent was affected by what happened during war, and how they respond to the family could have changed, as it did for Daisy. She claims that the atmosphere in the house was "tense" for a few weeks or months after her father would come back. He was quick to anger and "kind of had a temper, maybe was a little rougher on us, I guess," because he worried about them and wanted to know what they were doing and where they were going all the time.

Daisy says that she did not perceive the change quite as much as her older siblings, who remembered their dad being much more relaxed in the way he acted and responded to his family before the deployment than the way he was when he returned.

Frank, who was always elated when his dad would come home, claims that transition from a single to a dual-parent household is always difficult for his dad when he came home. "It's always like there's a vacuum of power even that you don't notice until that he gets back."

He remembers one particular experience when he was younger where he had to button a shirt a certain way and he was adamant that only mom knew how to do it, which he realized hurt his dad's feelings, but after months of only having his mom, he had forgotten that his dad knew how to do the task as well.

While Daisy's little sister, who was born while her dad was deployed, was too young to remember welcoming home their dad, that wasn't the experience Brandon and Lindsey's siblings had. For Lindsey, she remembers that her dad came home for a two-week R&R toward the end of a year-long deployment, but her preschool-aged little sister "didn't even recognize him because he had been gone so long and she was so young." This was difficult for the whole family, but she could see how much it pained her dad even more than having to miss out on the milestone moments from the year apart.

Brandon notes that his little brother had the same experience when their mom came home after deployment as she tried to kneel down and hug him, but her brother acted as though she was a stranger to him. Although she was hurt that her son did not rush into her arms right away, Brandon states, "she understood that dad was the only parent that my brother has seen when he was young." Brandon looks at the relationship that both he and his brother have with their parents and firmly believes his mom's military deployments explain why his little brother is closer to their father while he is closer to their mom.

CHANGES IN THE SOLDIER PARENT FOLLOWING A DEPLOYMENT

As mentioned before, home life was always tense when her father would return, but it was not until Daisy saw her dad, freshly home from his last deployment, start to enact changes in their home. Mostly concerning curfew and chores, basically being "stricter on certain things," was when she began to see what her older siblings already understood: war had changed their dad. While she tries her best to understand why these changes occurred, it is something that she, and many other forgotten conscripts, have to learn how to adjust to with the return of a soldier parent who is changed as a result of the time engaged in conflict downrange.

Frank, Lindsey, Zion, and Leslie also saw similar types of changes in their military parent after they returned from extended training or serving in a conflict region. Frank claims physical injuries his dad sustained while deployed started to make it harder for his dad to sleep, resulting in him being "really grouchy," and each time he leaves for another tour and returns "it becomes even worse."

Lindsey says her dad also has some issues with sleeping at night, so if he fell asleep on the couch and she or her sisters woke him up, he would become agitated if anyone disturbed him and yell at them—something her father never did before his deployment.

For Zion, he knows both his father and stepfather deal with symptoms of post-traumatic stress disorder (PTSD) because of what they endured while serving in a war zone. While his stepdad chose an introverted route, keeping more into himself and remaining quiet in most situations, Zion's dad found that he returned with a "short fuse and was quick to anger," which led him to have to make some changes in his life. He got more involved with his local church following his retirement from military service. While he says his father still has a "wicked temper" at times, prayer and his faith helped his dad to confront the emotional scars he carried with him from his time at war.

Leslie, whose story started this chapter, states that her dad used to be a kindhearted and giving man, but started to develop some severe changes in his personality upon his return home from deployment to Afghanistan. He would keep to himself, often sitting in the garage, playing video games, smoking cigarettes, and drinking heavily. She claims that these were "bad habits he had before, but when he came home, he was silent and just wanted to be left alone."

Her father also would be fixated on the safety of the home and the family, to the point that he would sit in the house with the lights off for hours and watch outside the windows for anyone who might do them harm. Her dad did not keep guns in the house, instead opting to have other weapons, like knives, hatchets, and swords, all over the house he would claim was "for protection." She recalls her dad would get up several times at night to check and recheck the locks on the doors and windows. It was almost like how a person with OCD worries about something to the point that they cannot focus on anything else.

It took them months of this type of behavior before Leslie's father would finally seek help for his pain.

When Leslie tried to talk with him about a year after he came back from deployment about how distant he had become, her father asked her to think about how many of her friends have actual fathers living at home with them.

"He told me, 'Well, you should be lucky that I'm here.' But what he does not realize like, yes, maybe physically but emotionally you are not here, so technically, I don't. I don't feel like I have a father anymore."

After he was diagnosed with PTSD and was getting treatment, Leslie says it helped at first, but she thinks he sometimes uses it as a crutch or an excuse for his choice. Instead of trying to talk or share his feelings, he would just claim that it was his PTSD like it was a catch-all for any bad behavior.

The shock of her father's decision to leave her and the rest of the family behind for a fresh start only served to intensify the feelings of abandonment that had developed in Leslie because of her experiences growing up as a forgotten conscript.

"It's like I never had a father figure," she says.

Chapter 6

Advantages and Aggravations within the Military Culture

He just wanted to be Romeo.

Assigned female at birth, Brandon, 16, knew from a young age that skirts were not in his future. When playing house with cousins, he always "wanted to be the dad or the brother or whatever," but never the female role.

When middle school came around, Brandon's school in the South had mandatory uniforms. When his mom, a sergeant in the Army, came home with the girls-style clothes that he realized "how uncomfortable [he] felt." Ever the adapter, Brandon didn't say anything and wore what she had bought. The next summer, with his new super short haircut, he made sure he went with his mom when she picked up the uniforms and got the "boy cut" he wanted.

In eighth grade, when the teacher used the pronoun "he" to refer to Brandon at a conference, his mom made a note and questioned him afterward. "She said, 'You didn't correct him,' so I told her it didn't really matter to me. She didn't say anything about it after that, but I think she understood then."

When ninth grade came, everything changed. He was still with the same kids, but as he watched the other guys' voices deepen as maturity hit, that was when people noticed the difference between Brandon and the other boys.

That was also when the bullying started.

What began first as comments and whispers turned into outright aggression and hurtful comments. Yet when a classmate yelled out, "You can't be Romeo because you're not a dude," and the teacher did not correct nor stop her from making a scene in class or allow him to be read the role of the Shakespearean lothario, he knew he would most likely never be accepted at that school.

Another time, a student used the pronoun "it" referring to Brandon, an experience he says "hurt his soul" in a way that still lingers today.

After finally surviving that horrific year, his mom got orders to come to a new duty station and, luckily, to a high school with a GSA (Gay-Straight

Alliance). From there, Brandon, who had just started testosterone that summer, was able to flourish as he made sure the school was aware of his new name and gender identity.

Aside from a few "curious students," Brandon was accepted in his new school with his chosen gender identity. He claimed the hardest part was having to remind teachers to use his preferred name as it would be too much red tape to legally change it until he is no longer a military dependent.

Reflecting on his transition, he sees how being a military-connected adolescent both helped and hindered his process. He was forced to remain in a school that was less than accepting because forgotten conscripts must be wherever their military parents are ordered to go. On the other hand, he also sees that all his previous experiences as a military brat gave him the tools to survive these experiences in a resilient way.

But if given the opportunity again, he would have stood up for himself and fought harder to be Romeo.

* * *

As with any other culture, there are both benefits and hindrances that come with membership. Forgotten conscripts endure various pluses like seeing the world and experiencing new people and countries while also enduring drawbacks like the ones Brandon experienced. Question any military brat and they will tell you that there is a healthy mix of both advantages and aggregations that come with being a forgotten conscript.

ADVANTAGES AND BENEFITS

Unless a family has considerable wealth, being able to live abroad is not a feasible option for most. Yet it is something routinely offered to military families. This is a major selling feature to young soldiers, but also a benefit in being able to share the world with loved ones.

While she was too young to remember much of Italy, Daisy states those memories from her older siblings and parents are often some of their favorites to share amongst one another. The family was able to visit historical destinations throughout Europe while stationed there that would have cost an unfeasible amount if the large family tried to pay out of pocket.

Brandon was also younger during his time stationed in Germany and although he did not have fond memories of the education system there—"they kept trying to make us sing Germany songs is the biggest memory I have"—his time abroad did awaken in him a desire to "explore and travel." This is something that he feels he will continue to pursue in the future.

For Frank, because he has traveled so much, both in the U.S. and overseas, it baffles him that families sometimes rarely leave the state they live in. At last count, his family has lived or visited over 30 states in the U.S. and 14 countries abroad. He recalled talking with a neighbor at this last duty station and when she explained she had only lived in three other states, "that blew [his] mind."

Being able to be a world traveler is something that Zion enjoys as well. He recalls being able to visit different countries but being able to see the Great Wall of China during his time in South Korea was the biggest highlight. Zion believes that his time in South Korea gave him a chance to interact with people from around the world, which enabled him to develop a mindset where "you don't see people differently," a trait that he did not always identify among his peers.

However, since his parents retired when he was much younger, Zion admits he is jealous of some of his fellow forgotten conscripts because of how often they got to visit new places.

Sage expressed a similar sentiment when his dad turned down orders for Germany because, in retrospect, he would have liked to have had the chance to visit Europe. He saw it as an opportunity that would probably not be afforded to him as an adult unless he joins the military like his father. Yet, he feels that he was still able to increase his open-mindedness through the exposure to diversity having lived in nearly all regions of the continental United States.

Lindsey claims that being able to live in multiple states while growing up allowed her to adjust her point of view on the world. Being able to travel, meeting new people, and learn from them benefits her in a way that often overshadows the obstacles she faced due to the high mobility of being in a military family. This is often where that empathy, part of the MACE identity forgotten conscripts learn to wield, is developed.

While difficulties moving is often a commonality among forgotten conscripts, many still see the benefits as they look at it more as an opportunity or simply a way of life and less as an obstacle. For Brandon, even though he struggled in some places, this routine part of his childhood meant he had the chance to start a new chapter in his life each time he moved. He claims that this is why he and his brother "don't really trip" when their mom comes home with new orders to move to a new military post.

As mentioned in chapter 4, a bonus to the high mobility means that forgotten conscripts might get the opportunity to circle back and revisit a previous place they had lived. Lindsey, Leslie, and Zion were all able to experience this and reflected that it did make the transition easier due to the familiarity with the duty station. This meant they did not have to start from scratch when they moved and could fall back in with old friends and familiar locations.

Daisy also moved several times during her childhood and claims that the long period of living in Virginia was the hardest growing up because they stayed in one place for so long. "I wanted to experience something new because I knew everyone there," she lamented.

Leslie states she would go through a process each time the family found out they were going to move. She would be sad to leave her friends and community behind, but after a few days, she would be filled with excitement as "it was always a new start." She laughs that sometimes when life felt dull, she would think to herself "Man, can dad just get orders, so we can PCS again?"

While the process of having to pack up an entire house each time can be exasperating, it also holds a promise of new adventures on the horizon for forgotten conscripts. This is one of the things Leslie says she misses the most since her dad retired from the military: they would never move again and be allowed to experience a fresh start in a new place.

AGGRAVATIONS AND FRUSTRATIONS

While it is easy to see the benefits, they do not diminish the taxing experiences that forgotten conscripts encounter. Some of these problems are fleeting—often subsiding after a short amount of time as the forgotten conscript acclimates to a new setting or scenario. Others can leave secret scars that hurt far beyond adolescence.

Even though moving can provide opportunities to see the world and embrace new experiences, this does not diminish the fact that moving so often is simply exhausting. "The constant moving is probably the worst thing because you get comfortable in a place and then you have to leave," Lindsey explains. "It's just like you meet people and everything's great, and then . . . you leave."

Daisy shares that while each duty station offers a variety of entertainment and destinations to visit—some are better than others. Her family most recently moved to the Midwest after only living either on the East coast or abroad, so the regional customs were "kind of weird" to the family at first. Also, to go from having a coastline to being landlocked was a culture shock, even though their parents "tried their best to help them integrate into the new community, it was still a hardship to have to leave behind something that you learned to count on."

Early summer and the winter holiday are when military families are given orders to move. Therefore, for years Elias feared the end of the school year because he remembers experiencing coming home only to get the bad news of having to pack up and move yet again. This is quite a different reaction from his civilian classmates.

It was the lack of control over when a move was going to be was far scarier for him than the actual move itself. While being able to adapt to any changes that come is part of his MACE identity, the lack of control over when these changes will come does make adjusting brutal at times.

Being the new kid in school can feel like being famous for a few days as it coincides with an increase in attention for military-connected adolescents. While some forgotten conscripts claim they liked the excitement, others felt that it just made for more opportunities to endure being ostracized or, even worse, bullied.

Although he did not perceive it at the time, Elias states that he often felt isolated when stationed in Texas as an elementary kid, because his new kid status left him without a good group of friends. In most situations, he felt like a third wheel or a tag-along as the circle of friends was already established, so it was like he was an afterthought for birthday invitations or being asked to play on the playground.

Frank claims that his pride in being linked to the military often brings him some unwanted attention, like some peers "scoffing" at him because he proudly wears his U.S. Army lanyard to school each day. However, the biggest experience he had with bullying was during his time in Europe from the German children and adults living near the base. On more than one occasion, he would hear civilians mutter "stupid Americans" in their direction when they would travel. This experience made him "even more appreciative" of the rights he has as an American.

Issues with trust and abandonment are common among forgotten conscripts. Both Lindsey and Leslie have severe issues in this way because of parental deployment and consistently having to cut ties with friends and communities because of the seemingly never-ending cycle of having to move every few years. Lindsey shares that these feelings have also impacted her ability to date. She claims she had difficulty getting close to a boyfriend one summer because she knew it would eventually have to end and that the relationship ultimately fizzled out.

For Leslie, this fear makes her more protective and apprehensive about opening up to new people as she worries that she will "get really close to people, like letting them in, and they'll just leave." Leslie's trust issues come from not only moving so often but also because her dad decided to remain emotionally and physically distant from the family after his return. As mentioned in chapter 5, her dad basically abandoned the family after his military retirement in favor of a new government contractor job and the new girlfriend.

Leslie fretted that her father, who failed to call her after her senior prom, even though she "kept reminding him," was going to not make it home to attend her high school graduation. This caused her anxiety to flare up in an already stressful situation. He did end up showing up for graduation but caught a flight back the very next day. "This feeling [of being] unwanted like that it makes me wonder, like is there something with me?" Leslie fears.

Perhaps one of the biggest aggravations is because the military dictates where a family will go, if the military-connected child finds themselves in a bad situation, like Brandon, there is no way to move away from it. A child being bullied in school could be pulled and put in another one or the entire family can move if there are concerns about the safety of the neighborhood or city. This action is inaccessible for most military families.

As pointed out earlier in the book, when Sage's dad was deployed during his 7th-grade year, he and his brother found themselves in a tough spot when the only person capable of caring for them was a soon-to-be distant family member. On top of that, even though his dad sent money to help with their care, it was not enough for the cost of living in Virginia, so they faced bullying for having to wear hand-me-down clothes. And while the time Sage spent away from his family helped him to develop empathy, which he identifies as a benefit as it "humbled him to learn to count his blessings," he still looks at the year in a negative light.

Leslie, who shares that she has been having a tough time in high school the past few years, dealing with issues of anxiety, bullying, and overcoming a sexual assault during her junior year, states that one of the hardest parts was that "you can't run away from these issues." The ability to leave the situation was not an option because her dad had orders to stay in this city no matter the problems his daughter faced.

No one understands this better than Brandon, whose story started this chapter. Deciding to transition from female to male in an unwelcoming environment was "simply the worst," but he never blamed his parents' role in the military for having to endure it. Having faced adversity and come out better on the other end made him believe that he would "probably just stay" anyways and deal with the issues versus running from them. This level of maturity makes it easy to see why it is a clear facet of a military-connected adolescent MACE identity.

SOURCES OF MILITARY-CONNECTED ADOLESCENT THRIVING

Thriving occurs when a person encounters an obstacle and not only survives but turns out better, as a result of their experience with adversity (O'Leary

& Ickovics, 1995). Most forgotten conscripts will agree that even though they experience hardship, they still view themselves and their military family positively and feel they are better prepared for the future. Or, as Frank puts it, forgotten conscripts and military families are simply "stronger than ordinary families" because of all they must endure.

One way military-connected adolescents perceive they can thrive can be attributed to the support they receive from their parents or guardians. Bailey states that when it comes to her and her sister, they "just understand each other," which helps her develop the confidence she needs to thrive. Elias shares that the consistent verbal support from his father about how proud he is of him makes it easier for him to develop resiliency in his life.

The support that Daisy perceives from her mother as she is "really good at making sure we have everything and that we feel like we're a part of [our dad's] life." This makes going through all the tough experiences that come with being a forgotten conscript much easier.

However, the one thing that virtually all military-connected adolescents perceive is unwavering parental support for whichever path they choose to follow into adulthood. Frank states many people often assume forgotten conscripts are going to follow in their military parent's footsteps and join the military. While this is an option many either plan to do or have seriously considered, Frank, like several others, states he feels he would be supported by his parents no matter the choices he makes. Knowing this helps Frank to see himself able to thrive despite the possibility of obstacles in the future.

Despite hardships, forgotten conscripts agree that the sacrifices their parents make on their behalf help them learn to thrive as military-connected adolescents. Zion's mother decided to retire from the military so they could "stay close to the family through his teenage years" while Sage's father asked him and his brother to choose which duty station they wanted to live for their final years of high school—a rare option for military families. The parental decisions made these young men feel as though they have some control over their lives.

It is important to note that is not just the military parent that sacrifices for the family. Both Elias and Leslie point out that the support of their home parent made it easier to thrive as part of the military culture. Elias is grateful that his mother is "tough" enough to handle the ups and downs of their lives, which include himself and his brother who "were a handful."

Leslie says that although she may not have recognized it when she was younger, she is grateful for the sacrifices her mom made for her and her brother during their childhood. Even though she often complains about the things her mother is unable to do for her because of her bouts of depression, Leslie still feels that she is successful in life because of her mother's support, which has helped her to develop a sense of independence.

Since it is just the family that military-connected adolescents can rely upon during tumultuous events, many feel this made their family grow closer as a result. Elias and Daisy communicate with their family members daily through group chats and family dinners. Zion also feels that the closeness he has with his parents is different than his peers who often do not feel as comfortable with their parents. He thinks of himself as close with his mom as a self-proclaimed "mama's boy," while he says he and his dad are "just alike," so he perceives they could "literally just chill all day."

Brandon expresses these same feelings of closeness with his mom, which he attributes to the fact that it was just the two of them when he was younger when they "did everything together basically," he claims. Being able to rely on the closeness of the family as a unit is one way many forgotten conscripts feel helps them learn to thrive while growing up within the military culture.

Supportive friends are another major source of resiliency for military-connected adolescents. Bailey claims that being able to find good friends at each new place was a lifesaver for her to take a deep breath and get through it all. Sage talks about how even though they may have moved, he keeps in touch with friends from previous duty stations, which is good on tough days to have people to talk to and work through his feelings.

Brandon claims that it was his JROTC family that helped him feel accepted and welcomed, not just as a new student, but through his gender transition. He found support among the fellow cadets, but he also saw it from the instructors of the program. When they began passing out uniforms, the instructor asked all the girls to stand up, and by instinct, Brandon stood. Not missing a beat, he states that the instructor said, "Were you not listening? I said girls," and just walked away, so Brandon sat down. Their immediate acceptance made not only the stress of moving subside but his fear about his transition being welcomed as well.

SOURCES OF PERCEIVED STRUGGLES WITH MILITARY LIFE

While most perceive the military lifestyle as a positive influence on them, not everyone sees their experiences as forgotten conscripts in that manner. For some of them, the military experience colored how they view their relationships with their soldier parent, their home parent, and their siblings.

Some forgotten conscripts identify a perceived disconnect with the military parent in their family because of the experiences the soldier encountered within the military culture. Sage claims that he still has respect and appreciation for his dad, yet still gets "frustrated or upset with him" when the authoritarian side of his dad comes out.

Zion also agrees and states that many people don't understand that "military parents are much harder than regular parents" because of the heavy authoritarian culture that runs throughout the military.

Lindsey claims that even though she and her father have "a pretty good relationship," she has some troubles getting her dad to try and understand the hardships she and her sisters have dealt with as military brats. She asserts that every time she tries to explain her feelings about a decision, her father will turn it back on her, claiming to not understand why she would feel that way and even calling her "ungrateful."

On the flip side, Lindsey explains that it feels like her dad has tried to live through her experiences as he used to force her to do things she might not want, like learning to play basketball in middle school. While that experience could have been one that brought them together, because she saw it as a way for him to "brag to others about her accomplishments," it became a negative experience for Lindsey, thus hurting their relationship.

For many, the lack of closeness to their military parent—physically and emotionally—left them feeling like they were living with a stranger. Regarding the relationship with his soldier father, Frank commented that he and his dad would "just function" together because he has been gone so often during his childhood.

Elias claims that he and his dad "kind of [were] used to all being alone in our own separate places" after having spent so much time apart. He is quick not to fault his father for this feeling of being disconnected, rather the family just learned how to be more self-reliant without him because of his continual absences.

For Leslie, the disconnect was not because her dad was not home, it's just that when he was there, they still didn't connect. After years of trying to reach out only to be rejected by a parent, Leslie developed unhealthy self-care issues and she often "forgets it is just as important to take care of yourself too." Even if that means cutting loved ones out of your life, she claims.

Even though it is the home parent forgotten conscripts ultimately spend more time around, that did not always result in the development of a strong relationship between parent and child. Brandon claims that he and his father are not "super close, we just kind of talk and that's it," as he is closer with his mom.

While Frank respects his mom, he talks about them having more of "a teammate relationship more than like a son-mother one" as they work to juggle the responsibilities of the home during his father's absence. While most would love that type of relationship, for Frank, it felt like he had to fill in as a pseudo parent and could not just be a kid growing up.

Daisy feels the problems that she has with her mom stem from the fact that they "have the same kind of personality" so they "kind of clash sometimes."

This means the parent she finds herself in trouble with most is her mother, which is not good when it is her soldier father that is absent more in the home, leaving the two to have to make it work.

Lindsey claims, as with Daisy, the similarities she has with her mom are the source of some of the strain she has with her. Yet, she claims the behavior comes from the control that her mom tries to exert over her life, which is getting worse as she approaches adulthood. Even though the rest of the family is set to move after she graduates from high school, Lindsey wants to attend college in their current state. Lindsey says that it took many months for her mom to finally accept that she would not follow them to their next duty station. This disconnect makes Lindsey seek out her dad, because even though she doesn't perceive their relationship as much better, at least he isn't "as dramatic" like her mom.

While the relationships any teen has with a parent are inevitably rocky, there are other factors that forgotten conscripts experience that civilians do not, which makes forming these relationships even more laborious.

Chapter 7

Coping Strategies for Forgotten Conscripts

If one does something enough, it becomes ordinary, which is how many military brats express the experience of being a forgotten conscript. At this point, they are old hats at being adaptable.

Sage readily admits that the relationship he has with his father is indelibly colored by the military culture. Between multiple deployments and duty stations over the years, Sage claims his father tries his best, but "he's just not always there." This is a running theme of his childhood but acknowledges that it was not always his father's choice.

While military-connected adolescents understand the demands of their soldier parent's profession to mean time away from home, many of them already deal with the military imposing long workdays, resulting in limited opportunities be together. Sage asserts this lifestyle did influence him after a while. "It's gotten to the point where it's just how life is going for me. It is like this became normal. I don't know how else to explain it." Moving, adaption, parental absence—they all feel like a natural rhythm of his life.

Since Sage's mother was not always there—and when she was, she was not always reliable—it meant he and his twin brother had to rely on their father. The problem is that because of his profession, Sage's dad was absent. A lot.

When they moved to their last duty station, his father had promised that he would finally have a normal 9–5 job, but still seems to be called in early and often asked to stay late. "We'd be lucky if he comes home before 7 p.m. sometimes. I mean, I know he has a job to do, but he's just . . . gone." While he says he feels comfortable going to his stepmom with problems, "there are sometimes I just need my dad."

On the other hand, Daisy, daughter of a Marine officer, claims she could feel the presence of her father even when he was not physically there. Everything they do reflects not just on them but him as well, so "there's definitely a pressure to support obviously the military in general and to make sure we're like not doing what we're not supposed to be doing," Daisy says.

Unlike Sage, Daisy feels blessed that their mother was there to help them go through the ups and downs of military life. Her mom is proud of being involved as a military spouse, often serving as a member of the Family Readiness Group designed to help support military families on base. This does not mean that her mom did not struggle. She is just better at hiding it, according to Daisy, who did not realize how much her mother did for her and her siblings until she was in high school.

One of ten children in the family, Daisy shares they had a family friend, Ms. Amy, stay with them during one of the times her father was deployed. While her presence helped to alleviate the stress in the home, it only intensified how different her family was from her civilian friends.

She remembers her mom kept the children involved in several different extracurricular activities while their dad was gone, including sports and church. While she knows now this added more stress to her mom to have to manage that schedule—especially since she gave birth to her little sister while their father was deployed—Daisy says she is grateful for her mother's sacrifice as it was easier for her and her siblings to cope with his absence and because it made the deployment go by faster.

* * *

Fight or flight is a natural human response to adversity. For forgotten conscripts who perceive their wings as clipped, forcing them to stay in one place until the military orders the family to fly to a new place, it is easy to see why the act of fighting back feels like a good option. Sometimes it is the only option.

There is a great need to better understand the coping strategies that military-connected adolescents use to survive their formative years. Forgotten conscripts develop different ways to cope and seek out support to help them learn to understand their role in the military, to survive their experiences, and even learn to thrive.

RELIGION

Finding sources of support is a vital resource for forgotten conscripts as they learn to cope with their experiences. Religion tends to be a place where solace is found as faith is something one can pack up and take with you.

Daisy states that her family's religion—Catholicism—is an important part of their identity as they devoutly attend church every Sunday. A major part of this stems from the fact that her father had plans of becoming a priest before he traded in his dream of wearing the cloth for a set of military BDUs. His faith was something he worked to instill in his children, Daisy claims, which helped her to cope during struggles in her life as a forgotten conscript.

Sage admits turning to prayer when he found himself feeling lost due to deployment or an upcoming move. Leslie and Brandon were both raised in religious homes but found themselves leaning more on the power of positive thinking and optimism over prayer. Optimism, which is a part of the forgotten conscripts MACE identity, evolves into a source of support for forgotten conscripts in these situations.

Frank, who also spoke at length about his family's connection to their church, states people may claim to understand the danger and hardships that come with this life, but they can only sympathize as they will never fully grasp the inherent fear military brats face:

> The biggest thing that people don't understand is with military parents, they could go to work and not come back. Going to bed every night praying that your dad is still alive. Even when they're just going to work—who knows there could be a misfire, especially in the range, there could be a misfire. Or they walk the wrong way two miles and then they got blown up by an artillery shell. And so, that's probably the biggest thing civilians do not understand. I think that's the last thing they'll understand.

Frank claims that his faith is the only thing he can always rely on when he starts to feel that worry creeps in.

SIBLING RELATIONSHIPS

The stress of the military culture can bring a family closer together, but the tightest bond tends to be the one between siblings in military families. Many would argue that the sibling bond is one of the most enduring ties teens experience, often linked to the development of a stronger sense of self and peace.

Daisy, who never found herself lacking in the presence of her nine siblings, says that the relationship she has with her sisters is strong, even with those who have moved out of the house. As a family, they talk almost every day which helps her to know she can rely on them.

For Leslie, the bond she has with her brother is the only one she perceives as always reliable. Leslie remembers that when she would wake up from a bad dream or felt upset, she could go to her brother for support. "When I was really scared, I would climb into bed with him over my parents," she shares. Even though he is much older and has not lived at home for years, she admits she sometimes still sleeps in his bed on tough days.

She recently got his name tattooed on her back in Japanese because she feels her "brother is literally my other half." Leslie says that although they had a typical sibling relationship and fought sometimes growing up, she knows she can always rely on him and views him as her past, present, and future protector.

Sage claims that his relationship with his brother was extremely close, not uncommon for twins, but he insists that having a brother to go through all these experiences as military-connected adolescents made it easier to cope. Sage claims he would have been lost if he had been an only child because it would feel like "I'm going through all this alone." Having a brother was like having a built-in friend who understood exactly was he was going through "because he was going through it just like me."

However, because the relationship with his twin is so close, it only intensifies the pain he has knowing that they have younger sisters from his mom's other relationships that they were unable to grow up with and do not know very well to this day.

This is not to say that being a part of a military family magically makes the sibling relationship better. While Lindsey stated that she had a tougher time dealing with expectations as the older sister in the family, she also finds herself dealing with feelings of jealousy between her and her sister as they relate differently to being part of the military.

The middle child in the family claims that she loves being a military kid, according to Lindsey. When the subject came up recently about moving yet again, her sister proclaimed she could not wait to move again. "I remember looking at her and saying, 'Girl, why?' because I could not understand how anyone could love having to pick up and settle somewhere as often as we had to," she expresses.

Additionally, her youngest sister is only five and with her father's military retirement right around the corner, Lindsey admits that she feels some jealousy that the baby of the military family will not have to have the same childhood that the older sisters did.

While she will still have to deal with an authoritarian parent because "my dad will always be my dad," Lindsey's baby sister will not have to experience the high mobility and parental absence she did. "She'll go to middle school with the same people and then go to high school and graduate with them, versus us." Although she recognizes growing up within the military culture gave her certain opportunities, the notion that Lindsey's younger sister will not have to deal with the same situations and obstacles as she does upset her, and she thinks it may have impacted their relationship.

COUNSELING

Sometimes talking to family or seeking support from a higher power is not enough to help forgotten conscripts to work through the emotions they are feeling. That means they need to turn to a professional counselor for help and direction.

Religion helped Sage work through difficult times of being a forgotten conscript, but when his dad deployed during early adolescence, he felt so confused and lost that even his twin brother could not get through to him.

He claims that he tried to "just let it out and talk about it," but found he did not know what to do once he started to let it go. He eventually talked with his "aunt," his caregiver at the time, about seeking help. Real help.

While he only spoke with the counselor once, he did find that talking about his issues with someone who could help him navigate those emotions was a useful coping tool. He admits he now has begun talking with his dad, his teachers, and even his brother when he finds himself dealing with something difficult.

EXTRACURRICULAR PARTICIPATION

Coping with moving into a new school is made easier when the forgotten conscripts join with clubs, sports, or other extracurricular activities. They use these groups to help them find friends and to have a place to escape the stress of being a military brat, or as an opportunity to feel accepted in their new setting.

Finding a connection with people in school through extracurricular activities helps Daisy to meet new people each time she moves. Lindsey uses her time working on the school newspaper to meet people who have similar interests and passions and could escape into that club when she was feeling stressed. Leslie also found that to be true and joined several leadership and social clubs in high school to help her feel more connected and to give her purpose as she felt she "needed something else in [her] life."

Elias looks to clubs like JROTC to help him find a place to belong and feel like he is a part of something he views worthwhile. As an upperclassman, Elias served in a leadership role in JROTC, which gave him pride, but he realizes that his experiences as a military-connected adolescent set him up to handle the stress of such a huge responsibility.

Sports is the avenue of choice for Sage, Zion, and Bailey to find connections and support growing up. With cross country, basketball, and track, Sage played sports year-round to keep him active and maintain peer relationships.

Zion, who claims to not "do a lot of extra activities," said that football was a big part of his time in school, and the best way he found to meet people it was "basically how I met all my friends."

Athletics is a great way to help forgotten conscripts find a quick way to connect and become part of a school when they move. This is something Bailey agrees with as sports participation is a given when she finds herself in a new school setting.

She remembers her first day at this latest school, walking around with her tray at lunch like something out of a bad after-school special, only to hear a fellow volleyball player she had just met at practice call her over. While playing sports helped her meet people, she also called it her "getaway," as it helped to funnel her focus on the sport and gave her an outlet to forget the stress of being a forgotten conscript.

Frank, who also used sports and extracurriculars to integrate into a new school, found clubs outside of school help him find acceptance. As a Boy Scout, Frank knew that friends could be found the moment he located the closest troop at each new duty station. Being a member of this organization helps him to find friends and gives him a place to keep his mind off the worry that came each time his dad was gone.

Brandon also used outside clubs like Kudos, a local chapter of a black youth fraternity, as a means of developing relationships. This acceptance, especially being a part of the male group as a trans man, was a huge confidence boost and made him feel like this new duty station would be a positive one.

EDUCATORS FOR SUPPORT

Forgotten conscripts who perceive the school they were in as welcoming found their teachers and counselors solid sources of support to help them deal with the struggles of growing up as a military-connected adolescent. These adults become listeners, confidants, and advocates for military kids.

Bailey expresses she had some apprehension before she moved to her current school, but that the teachers made the transition smoother. Knowing that if she had a problem, she could rely on her teachers for help makes her feel better, which she believes helps her to "work harder than [she] used to." This support resulted in improved grades, ending her time in high school on a strong academic note.

Daisy also feels that her elementary schools were a great source of support while her father was deployed, which made the experience easier. She remembered that because the community has a strong military presence, they had assemblies in school to talk about what was happening and make sure the students knew the school supported them. Daisy acknowledges that the understanding of the communities she has lived in has been helpful for her and her family to cope with the experience.

When Sage lived in Virginia, he had a chance to experience what it is like to be in a school that did not have a strong military presence. He could feel the difference in support when he was at schools that were not near a military community because he felt less understood by the school in terms of being part of the military culture. Sage, and his other fellow military-connected adolescents, feel more schools need to recognize that they have forgotten conscripts who often feel left out in school—especially those not close to a military base like the children of National Guard or Reserve soldiers.

Brandon, on the other hand, states that even though he always lived in communities near military posts, there was a clear distinction between those who supported forgotten conscripts and those who did not. He had attended school districts that had military liaisons and helped him to find his classes and feel welcome on his first day. He also has been in schools where "nobody really kinda helped us, so I had to figure it all out on my own on that first day."

Brandon did say that some of the responsibility does fall on the military-connected adolescent to speak up and inform their teacher that they are "not just coming from another school" but are new because of their connection to the military culture. He thinks that if more teachers knew that their new students were military-connected adolescents, it could be more advantageous and welcoming for forgotten conscripts.

DETACHING FROM EMOTIONS

One way several forgotten conscripts claim to cope with the stress of the military culture is to simply tune it out and isolate themselves from those feelings. Many utter things like "I'm used to it now," or "It doesn't faze me," because they have learned to accept the unpredictable nature of this life as a part of who they are.

The hardest experience for most military-connected adolescents is parental absence due to training or military deployment. While many families grow up in single-parent homes, there is a difference for those who are doing so as part of the military culture as opposed to other circumstances. Children who grow up without a parent get used to only have one, but if you *do* have a second parent who lives with you, but "you don't know if they're ever going to come back," this causes extra anxiety for them, according to Leslie. However, focusing on these feelings constantly, according to Lindsey, "wasn't a good thing," so they must find ways to detach from those feelings to get by.

Brandon agrees and claims that not only is it unhealthy to worry all the time, but there is also this unspoken need to have to stay strong for their soldier parent in an attempt to make it easier for them to deal with being gone. He remembers that before his mom would leave for training, they often "look in each other's eyes" and he feels this desire to reflect the strength he always saw from his mom. Brandon insists holding back the emotions he felt as a military-connected adolescent is part of the unspoken duty of being a supportive child for his military parent.

Daisy also felt that the emotion she expressed needed to match what she thought she experienced when compared to other military-connected adolescents. While she experienced the hardships of deployment, her father came home relatively the same. Daisy acknowledges there is a greater "emotional toll obviously for people whose parents come back differs/ Maybe they lost a limb or, god forbid, their parent has died and now they have to deal with it." As such, she feels that she always must check her emotions because she knows others suffer far worse than she ever did.

As mentioned previously, Elias claims he has difficulty showing and attributes his disconnect to simply growing up in a culture that values stoicism. "It's just kind of like the flu or something. . . . you build an immunity and eventually you just get used to it and I feel like that's the same thing," he explains.

While most would think suppressing or detaching from their emotions is a negative thing, Elias views developing this skill in a positive manner because it allows him to remain calm in stressful situations and develop better self-control, which he perceives as being a benefit for him as a future adult.

ADVICE FOR OTHER FORGOTTEN CONSCRIPTS

In the same way siblings look out for one another, it is a hidden rule the military-connected children do the same for their fellow forgotten conscripts. Since no one understands this life until they have lived it, it is important for adolescents in this culture to offer words of advice to help others navigate the minefield of growing up military.

In terms of high mobility, Lindsey claims that the best thing to help feel settled is to find one thing and make it your own. For her and her sisters, that was their individual bedrooms. "I think setting up my room is my favorite thing about moving," Lindsey states. "I get to decorate it how I want to and make it feel really inviting and cozy for myself. I feel like that's like the one place that doesn't change. When I move, it's always going to be *my* space." Having a refuge that felt familiar and comfortable made it easier to overcome anything else that might be going on.

While most forgotten conscripts perceive themselves as extroverts, they also feel being bold, brave, and forward makes it easier to start over in a new place—even if that means they must force themselves to do it. Bailey, who was admittedly the shiest of all the ones interviewed, knew that she was going to have to push herself out there if she was going to survive in each new school setting. While she knew it would require her to come out of her comfort zone, Bailey feels this forced extroversion allowed her to meet more people and enjoy her time as a forgotten conscript.

Zion says forgotten conscripts should "try to be outgoing" because it can reduce the stress that comes from being the "new kid" and having to find new friends. After all, if you are shy, "then your high school life is probably going to be boring, honestly." Finding ways to fit in and find "your people"—be it forgotten conscripts or not—is essential for those in the culture.

While Lindsey claims that her general plan when she moves into a new town and school is to "wing it," the one piece of advice she would give forgotten conscripts is to start small when trying to find their place in a new setting, to not feel so overwhelmed. She claims she often tries to find at least one friend, one person she reaches out and talks with, and "then branch off from there." Daisy also feels that trying to just make one friend on that first day of a new school is a good goal and a great way to cope with the stress of being the new person in the class.

Trying new things is also an excellent way to help make the experience of being a military-connected adolescent easier, according to Frank. While his extroverted personality makes it more effortless to meet new people, he says that simply exploring a new place and looking for new experiences helps to make this life more exciting.

Brandon agrees with Frank and encourages students to realize that military-connected adolescents have much to offer if they are willing to try new things. "Don't feel like you're not up to where everybody else is at because you just moved here," he claims. "You already got that resiliency in you. . . . you keep working for it, it doesn't matter how far you think it's away from you." As Brandon explains, the ability to overcome any situation is already a part of who they are at their core, forgotten conscripts just need to remember that fact when they find themselves in difficult situations.

It is the reality that they have experienced so much and been exposed to the diversity of the world at a higher level that helps forgotten conscripts model empathy and open their hearts more to others, Leslie claims. They can be good role models for peers on how to care for others.

Sage encourages military-connected adolescents to remember that while they have the power to adapt to changing situations, one thing that should *not* change is who they are on the inside. He claims the best thing they can do is be themselves, because "at the end of the day, there's going to be people that you encounter [who] don't care about the person you are . . . so, the most important things to be yourself."

Sounds like solid advice for *any* adolescent.

Chapter 8

The Lasting Impact of Growing Up Military

Like bumping your head on an open cabinet—some things are destined to leave a mark. Being a forgotten conscript is one of them.

As a military brat himself, Elias' dad claimed he never really got to spend time with his own soldier father. This left him to grow up on the hard-knock streets of California until he found himself at the Army recruiter's office, so "he wants us to have what he never really got as a military child," Elias says.

This also resulted in deliberate and honest discussions about moves his father planned as Elias' dad wanted him and his younger brother to be aware of every choice he made during his 20-year military career. There were sacrifices on his father's part—even electing to forgo uprooting the family for a year when new orders put their dad at a base an hour away. His dad decided to go alone and drive home on the weekends. "It was tough, you can imagine, and he tried to put up a good front for us, but you could see it was hard."

Elias' dad tried to prepare him for what it would be like to "be the man of the house" before his father's first deployment because he remembered clearly what that experience was like. "That had a big impression on me—the role of having an obligation to my mom and younger brother. I want to make it more stress-free for them and be someone they could look up to since our father was not there." As a result, Elias feels as though he grew up to be tougher than his civilian peers.

Many believe military-connected adolescents are "forced to join" the service, and while this is a commonality among many military families, it is not a requirement. Yet Elias felt the draw to serve his country—just as the men in his family before him—from a young age.

During his time in high school, Elias was an active member of the JROTC program, becoming a leader during his senior year. While he fell short of being able to get into an elite military academy—something he dreamt of for years—his academics and work ethic earned him a spot in a rigorous ROTC program at an East Coast university, so he will become an officer in the Army after he finishes his undergraduate degree.

While the mark left from growing up military was something Elias could see early on, it took Bailey until she graduated from high school to understand the impact. Electing to leave her mother's care to live with her older soldier sister was a difficult choice for Bailey, but one she stresses gave her the stability she needed during her adolescence.

Twelve years her senior, Bailey's sister moved out when Bailey was young. This was when she realized that it was her sister that brought her comfort, guidance, and clarity and not her mom. "Since I was little, my sister took me under her wing. If I had to pick one person I could not live without, it would be her."

While it was hard to move away from her mom and little sister, she states it was the best decision as her mom did not value education or push Bailey to make better decisions. When her sister became her legal guardian, her school attendance and grades improved. Bailey claims she is so grateful that her sister agreed to take her because they know "what their family is like" and how easily she could have turned out aimless just like their mother.

While her sister was active in ROTC in college and knew the military would be her future, Bailey was reluctant to follow in her footsteps. After high school, she attended college in Texas, but that only lasted a year before Bailey joined the service herself. She states that "being able to grow up as a military kid made me a better person," and that translated into wanting to continue down this path as a soldier in her own right.

* * *

Membership in a culture equally influences and impacts a person on both conscious and unconscious levels. The military culture is no different—just ask any forgotten conscript. While most military-connected adolescents admit they internalize characteristics of the culture, most will admit that as they approach adulthood, growing up within this culture leaves a lasting mark that is undeniable.

IMITATING MILITARY VALUES IN DAILY LIFE

Since it makes such an impression on the military family and forgotten conscripts, it is only natural that family members would start to emulate the traits they see used or exemplified in the regimented lifestyle of the military culture.

As shown in chapter 2, military-connected adolescents perceive themselves as more mature than civilian peers because of the increased self-reliance, discipline, and respect they personify. Daisy takes it a step further by saying it has to do with an understanding of what is expected of them in any given situation as "there's a time to be professional and then there's a time to be crazy and there has to be a difference between them." Just like any teenager, forgotten conscripts are not mature all the time, yet they have a better grasp on how they are supposed to behave and have the self-discipline to follow through.

Frank feels imitating discipline is something many military-connected adolescents express nonverbally as well. In fact, that is the thing that makes it easier for follow forgotten conscripts to recognize one another. "If I see a student standing at ease [a military formation position] even though I know they haven't been to basic training, that's enough to tell me that they are affiliated somehow." According to Frank, this is often the way he was expected to stand when his soldier father was disciplining him. This mimicking of their soldier parent—whether it is taught to them or not—is a clear imitation of military culture.

Another obvious sign of being raised around the military is the concept of time management and punctuality. Following a set schedule and learning to manage time wisely was one of the first things Elias states he learned from his military father. There is a common adage among the military culture that you should be 15 minutes early because if you come on time, you are already late. Zion states that he even started to use the 24-hour clock that is used by the military on his phone because it was used so often at home.

However, the use of military language and lingo in the home is still the most common emulation of military life. Elias, who is also expected to use the military lexicon in JROTC, found he uses it despite the confused looks from his civilian friends. His JROTC and forgotten conscript friends would use it so much that he laughed at how much it "sounds like I'm actually in the military."

Frank found he uses military lingo and phrases in the Boy Scouts as they use similar language. These skills allowed him to fit in easier than his troop mates that did not have a military background. One time an adult leader used military phrases to explain something, and he remembers that when the leader walked away, they all looked at Frank to translate what he said. "I was like 'alright look, we just have to line up right there. He wants us in bed by eight o'clock, we wake up at six.' And the other kids were like 'he could've just said that?'" Frank laughed.

Most forgotten conscripts claim that their inclusion in the military culture helps them in other areas of their daily lives. It also helps them to feel more connected to the military culture in general.

MILITARY CULTURE AS A FACET OF IDENTITY

According to Elias, "everything that happens in your life, the good and the bad, it all defines who you are as a person." For forgotten conscripts such as himself, growing up as a member of the military culture has made a deep impression on who they eventually grow up to become.

While he sees that there are other cultures he belongs to along the lines of race and religion, he does not perceive them as being as impactful on his development being a forgotten conscript. In fact, he calls this experience "transformative" and that it can help military-connected adolescents "go from being one person to a better person." This perspective helps him to better understand who he is, the choices he has made in his life, and to continue to reflect the image he has in his mind of what members of the military culture should be.

Sage agrees that growing up within this culture is not something outsiders would view as "normal," but that is some of what makes it so influencing on the identity of forgotten conscripts. The unique nature of military service and military structure makes it harder for youth to separate it from who they are at their core.

This idea was something that Daisy expressed when explaining the difference between her and her civilian peers. At each duty station, she would encounter friends who had maybe been on post but did not really understand what happens to those who grow up on one and the expectations that come from being the child of a soldier. It is a culture shock for her civilian friends each time she explains the expectations for her and her siblings.

Most adolescents know their parents have a career but understanding that the family often takes on the military culture as a part of who they are is too foreign of a concept for outsiders to understand. Where a civilian parent who is a nurse, a plumber, or a lawyer can separate their work and home, a military parent's career takes priority over every person and every decision made in a military family. There is no escaping it and the impression that it ultimately has on who you are.

MILITARY FAMILY AS A GREAT PLACE TO GROW UP

Coming of age in a military family can be beneficial due to the better opportunities that come with being a part of the military culture. Sage, Leslie, and Bailey all spoke about how they perceive their military home life as more stable in terms of consistent and reliable income, housing, and access to healthcare.

Although most forgotten conscripts have no real knowledge of the difference between a civilian and military household, Sage and Bailey have experienced both, so their opinions come from the first-hand experience. Sage, who lived with a distant relative during his dad's deployment, also remembers living with his mom, who had "lower-end jobs," when they were little, so money was tight and structure and stability for him and his brother were lacking. Being a military-connected adolescent was not easy, but for Sage, he feels it "opened the door for me to see a bunch of ways of life."

Bailey mirrored Sage's response; living with her sister affords her stability she knew she would not likely receive if she remained living with her mother and younger sister. Bailey also points out that beyond the permanency her sister gives her, the gains that she has seen in terms of her academic potential have made life more beneficial growing up as a forgotten conscript.

On the other hand, Leslie states that while she enjoys the stability, the trade-off of having to deal with absent parents and anxiety from the unpredictable lifestyle almost makes it not worth it some days. Almost.

While it would be easy to complain about the hardships of growing up military, most do not try to mollify military life through hyperbole and admit that while it is mostly good, it does not alleviate the hardships they experience. "This hard life isn't for everyone," Elias stated. Daisy points out that growing up as part of a military family can clearly be difficult, especially considering the size of her family, but despite these difficulties, the opportunities that came from being part of this culture make it worth it.

Zion couldn't agree more with Daisy about how being a military-connected adolescent was a positive experience for him and one he thinks he might like his own children to grow up in. While he decided not to join after high school, he still admits "it would be a good way to start a family." Bad situations are unavoidable, people have rough lives all over, so at least the military "can set you up for life," making it the better option, in the long run, Zion claims.

CHOICE OF MILITARY AS A FUTURE CAREER

While forgotten conscripts overwhelmingly agree the military will always be a facet of their identity and a prolific part of their childhood history, when it comes to whether or not their relationship with the military will continue beyond adolescence comes in three options: a confident yes, an adamant no, or a maybe for various reasons. For each of them, their perception of, and reaction to their military-connected adolescent experiences weigh heavily in their decision.

Zion, Frank, and Elias see military service as the path they want to follow into the future. All three feel that following in their parents' footsteps makes sense and want to take it up a notch by setting their aim for some of the more elite jobs in the armed forces.

The least steadfast of the three, Zion believes his powers of perception and attention to detail will serve him well by focusing on criminology and that a degree in that field will help with a career in the FBI. He claims he never once felt as though his parents were forcing the military on him. While he trusts in this plan for criminology, he was hesitant to include the military option after high school. Instead, he elected to focus on being a barber to help him pay for college, something that he found easy considering the strong work ethic he developed as a forgotten conscript.

Frank, whose hard work and diligence allowed him to graduate high school a semester early, elected to follow in his father's footsteps. The tradition of military service is substantial in his family—he makes the 4th generation to serve in the Army. He hopes one day to be an Army Ranger, one of the more rigorous positions in the military's ground fighting force. The unique skills and training he will receive in these schools should serve him well in cybersecurity—a career path he hopes to work towards, but he firmly believes that the discipline he learned growing up as a military-connected adolescent is what will help him find success in the future.

For Elias, he planned to merge both college and the military from the start by applying for a military academy. Sadly, this plan did not come to fruition. These academies are difficult to get into, but his advanced placement classes and work in JROTC did help him get recognized by a top college ROTC program. While the military as a final career might not be his first choice as he is majoring in engineering, he does feel an obligation to serve his country no matter what and will be an officer after he finishes his degree. "You don't have to serve your whole life in the military; you just give a little bit of your time to at least contribute to something of our country," he claims.

Elias believes that the structure and discipline instilled in him as a part of a military family will follow him into his life as an adult. "Besides," he said, "you already have a job when you get out of school. So, you don't even have to look for a job afterward," which is a plus for him.

Often the reaction a forgotten conscript has to their experiences within the military culture is going to highlight how much they want to continue their affiliation after adolescence. As both Lindsey and Leslie found themselves dealing with heightened anxiety and depression due to her experiences in the military culture, it only makes sense that these two could not wait to watch military life recede in their rearview mirror as they drive as far and as fast in the other direction.

Leslie states that she will miss the monetary and healthcare benefits that come with being a military family, but not nearly enough to continue to remain a part of the culture as an adult. "Having a person leave you that you love so much and then you leave me as one person [only to come] back as a different one . . . I don't know if I want to go through that again," she asserts.

She admits she cannot control who she will fall in love with and marries, and staying in this military community where she graduated high school to attend college means the likelihood of meeting a soldier does increase. Leslie likes that the experiences she already had as a military-connected adolescent means she "knows how [she's] going to deal with it," if her heart does lead her back to this life. For right now, she is content going to college, working on her skills as a nail technician, and continuing to be a sexual assault activist following her attack during high school.

For Lindsey, who sees her entire childhood as a cycle of packing and unpacking her life, she sees her future being the exact opposite of what she experienced growing up as a part of a military family. "It's a good experience to have but at the same time, I don't want my kids to have to pick up and start over every few years," she states, "I want them to be able to grow that friendship and foundation with people."

In contrast to Leslie, Lindsey knows that even if the man of her dreams shows up, if he is a soldier she is going to walk away because the emotional toll this life had on her growing up is too much for her to even contemplate living through it again. For now, she is attending college, joined a historically Black sorority, and was asked to serve in a leadership role at school, all of which she claims is because of the development of her military identity.

As for Bailey, Sage, Daisy, and Brandon, they all contemplated how the military might be a part of their lives as they head out into the adult world but ultimately opted to take a wait-and-see approach for various reasons after high school.

Both Bailey and Sage could see themselves joining the service and living the life of a soldier while they were in high school, but only Bailey decided to forgo textbooks for a set of combat boots after her first year of college. It was her sister's service that ultimately made her want to give back and her selfless identity as a forgotten conscript inspired her to become a medic in the military. In fact, Bailey just came back from her first deployment downrange and is contemplating making her service a full-time career.

While Sage can see the benefits he has been afforded to be a forgotten conscript, he is still too hesitant to follow this path. Sage claims he and his twin brother have talked about the military as an option in the future and they both agree that it would only be a last resort to help pay for school and even then, they would join the National Guard first because "if I only have to show up for one weekend a month, that sounds like a good deal." They decided to go to a university in the same state that their soldier father retired so they could be close to him—finally being able to make the connections that they couldn't when their father was on active duty. They are majoring in business and have also cultivated leadership roles on campus just like Lindsey.

While serving the military as a soldier is not something Daisy would ever want to do, the idea of following in her mother's footsteps and becoming a military spouse is something she believes she would enjoy and feels she would be good at. Daisy claims that she would be nervous to raise a military family of her own after thinking about all her mom went through, but she is curious if she would approach it the same as her mother did as she sees herself having more of her dad's qualities. Daisy wonders how the stress of this life would affect her in the parent role as opposed to the child role. For the time being, she is enjoying college and her steady boyfriend . . . who happens to not be a soldier.

Brandon's decision about his future in the military has been an evolving one. While he asserts he grew up thinking the military would be the best path for him by joining JROTC and watching his parents serve, the reality of being transgender has forced him to reevaluate if the military is the best option. Or even an option at all.

As Brandon points out, under the Trump administration, transgender soldiers who were serving were being targeted with policies ranging from forcing them to serve under the gender they were born with to even removing them all together while those who want to sign up are being turned away from military service completely. That rejection is something he is not ready to experience.

Brandon had a difficult senior year that caused him to seek guidance from professionals who could help him understand his gender transition. Eventually, he decided he would instead focus on college first and, like Zion, improving his skills as a barber and working on his rapping. Either way, he believes that the military has had a positive impact on his life and that he will miss the respect and pride he has experienced watching his parents serve.

Whether they decide to follow the same path as their military parents or elect to traverse a completely opposite one, forgotten conscripts all agree that their time growing up in the military culture changed them in a way that will influence them for the rest of their lives.

Chapter 9

Implications for Educators of Forgotten Conscripts

While forgotten conscripts encounter both negative and positive experiences throughout their childhood, one of the hardest things about this life is the fact that civilians simply do not understand what it is like to live within the stronghold of the military culture.

Obviously, outsiders can recognize the hardships that come from frequent moves and sending a parent off to war, yet forgotten conscripts feel people tend to place too high of an importance on the fun and excitement that they think comes with the military lifestyle. They wish more would understand that while military kids recognize the privilege that comes from being a part of this life, it is "not all glitter and gold. You still have some limitations and some things that normal kids that live in a normal, ordinary life don't get," Sage claims.

Forgotten conscripts pay for the perks that people perceive come from this lifestyle. Many civilians do not understand the pressure that is naturally a part of this way of life, such as the worry over where they might live the following year or how different their parents will be when they return from a deployment. Or if they will return at all.

While they view themselves as adaptable, it still is not enough for them to wash away the feelings of being the outsider every time the soldier parent is told to pack up the family and head out for a new destination. In fact, sometimes forgotten conscripts are hesitant to open and reveal their outsider identity. Being accepted and appearing "normal" is the goal for many military-connected adolescents.

For instance, Brandon claims he sometimes just says he is from Florida when people would ask him at a new school and not tell people he is a military child at all. This was not because he was ashamed of his identity, but that sometimes it was "too much to explain" each time he was the new kid in school.

So, the question remains: how can educators and schools work to help support these students so they do not remain forgotten? Here are three major implications based on the material in this book should help to better inform teaching and learning among the members of this culture.

BETTER IDENTIFICATION WITHIN PUBLIC SCHOOLS

Schools must have ways to better identify military-connected adolescents to meet their needs. While it has become routine to collect basic demographic information on students including race, ethnicity, and gender, parental military status is not even collected let alone on the radar.

Military status can be divided up into an easy check of the box to indicate active duty, National Guard, Reservist, or veteran. This could help educators quickly see which students have a connection to the military and to what extent.

Understanding the military affiliation is vital. For example, children of a veteran might have already experienced parental absence, whereas a child of an active-duty soldier might not have experienced that yet. This can help educators to better understand the home life of their forgotten conscript students.

Those who live close to major military installations are often better identified as mandatory federal aid cards are sent home for parents to fill out annually. Started back in the 1950s, the federal aid program was intended to help compensate schools that see potions of their population migrate, like those near military installations. Using this data, schools can easily work to ensure that it is part of the information provided to educators. However, since this is not a mandatory requirement in most school districts, the data is often not cataloged and shared.

For the children of National Guard and Reservists, their connection to the military and support services embedded in the culture is limited. They often do not live near a military post, so finding fellow forgotten conscripts who understand this culture is often not a realistic option. This is even more apparent when their soldier parent is activated and taken from the home, forcing the family to have to navigate this experience all alone. These are the most overlooked among the forgotten conscripts, which is why *all* school districts should adopt a way to identify military-connected students and learn how to properly support them.

PROFESSIONAL DEVELOPMENT FOCUSED ON SERVING FORGOTTEN CONSCRIPTS

Helping to shape behavior, attitude, and value among students and teachers is a common goal in education. Teachers are taught to differentiate their lessons to reach all students. Therefore, professional development is a vital component to make sure educators stay abreast of the latest data and skills available to help teach forgotten conscripts.

Currently, little to no professional development addresses the needs of forgotten conscripts, even in school districts with a strong military presence. In fact, less than 10% of teachers report being specifically trained to work with military-connected children and under 50% have had any training at all (Kranke, 2019). Professional development on military-connected students should be an annual part of the back-to-school process educators go through each fall.

Over a decade that I have taught in a school district with more than a 25% of the student population being military-connected in some fashion, there has never been a specific professional development related to military-connected students. Not once.

Multicultural education is already a staple of preservice teacher education as it aids in the understanding of cultural conditioning and learning preferences among different groups. Adding relevant information about forgotten conscripts within a frame of multicultural education could help aid preservice teachers learn more about the identity, stressors, and particular challenges of military-connected adolescents.

There are several professional organizations including the Military Child Education Coalition that provide low-cost and even free professional development training for schools. Information and services are readily available from this group yet are infrequently utilized. Their workshops cover all ranges of K-12 by educating, advocating, and collaborating to resolve education challenges associated with the military lifestyle, according to the group's mission statement.

Another important thing is to ensure that all education and licensed professional counselors in public schools are trained on how to help support forgotten conscripts. Students like Sage who needed to talk with someone about the trauma he was experiencing during his father's deployment should not have to rely on outside counselors when there are ones already in the school. The military culture and military deployments are not going away, so this is something that is needed now and well into the future.

Forgotten conscripts need to feel connected to a school to help aid the transition after each move. Schools, especially those not near military bases, must have a strong support system for military-connected adolescents. This can be in the form of Student 2 Student organization—a Military Child Education Coalition program—or establish a buddy system for incoming military kids at every school.

One thing schools outside of major military installations have tried is to create a welcome packet specifically designed for forgotten conscripts. This information can help military families feel more connected to their schools and they can also help them to locate local resources that will help them become a part of the community. Packets like these can also have important information about the district, names of people within the school that are best equipped to help support the needs of forgotten conscripts, and anything else a military family might need when moving into the new community.

It would also be a great way to be able to take a quick assessment and collect information about the student's nonacademic factors. While demographic information is important, it is also vital for educators and administrators to understand the experiences that a military-connected student might have had before coming to this school as it can impact their success. This is probably most beneficial in a school with a smaller military presence as it will help to make sure those students are less isolated, and that their needs as forgotten conscripts are met.

Schools need to be ready to address other physical, mental, or emotional problems that are getting in the way of academic and social success of the students. This needs to be something that is not just an idea left up to individual states but a federal mandate that counselors on campus are trained to deal with military kids and educators are given the vital professional development needed to support this invisible population.

REINFORCE AND GROW RESILIENCY

While the military-connected adolescents perceive themselves as "outsiders," they share common experiences, beliefs, and perceptions that unite them. And as they appear resilient and confident on the outside, they are often taught to mask feelings of insecurity and isolation on the inside. While these feelings can lead them to seek out fellow forgotten conscripts as friends, it would be advantageous if military-connected adolescents had allies outside of the military too.

Teachers can help support military-connected students by listening to their needs, being patient as they adapt to the new school rules, and reinforcing structure and security within the classroom. Open communication with both the student and the parents could help anticipate changes in behavior that might come from an impending move or parental deployment.

This type of communication is more prevalent in elementary schools than the secondary ones, which is understandable. Younger children have a harder time understanding and navigating the experiences of being in the military culture, but that does not diminish just because they get older. Secondary students, especially those within the military culture, need to feel and see that support to prosper as well.

As with any other students, military-connected adolescents want to be seen and recognized for the things that make them unique. Granted, all schools might not have a large enough population to throw a military student appreciation day or start a Student 2 Student club, but that doesn't mean schools can't do these things in small ways.

Counselors and administrators who know a military child is set to move to a new location could pass along the card to the student's teacher(s) for them to sign or give them a T-shirt or photo of the school so that way they can be remembered (Astor et al., 2015). Lots of times people think they need to do something big but sometimes it's the small things that impact in a big way.

Below is an adapted list from *The Administrators Guide for Supporting Students from Military Families* (Astor et al., 2015) with strategies that schools can use to create a learning environment that is sensitive to the needs and worries embedded among membership within this culture:

- Maintaining a routine during parental deployment or if the soldier parent has come back seriously injured is key. Schools should allow the student time to discuss and answer any questions the military child might have, yet it is important to try to learn to return to a normal classroom routine as soon as possible. The worst thing a school can do is ignore when something tragic has occurred outside of the school setting for military-connected students.
- The school nurse should be aware of every military-connected adolescent as often youth will complain of a health issue, like a headache or feeling nauseous, that is not necessarily true because they simply are not addressing the worries or trauma that they have experienced because of this culture. This will help the nurse to better understand and support military students when they are not feeling at their best.
- Each and every school should have a display that shows respect, reverence, and honor for the armed forces and the sacrifices that they make. It could be a basic military appreciation display or one that showcases educators with their own military connection, be it service or being a forgotten conscript when they were young themselves. This can easily be something forgotten conscripts realize is also for them as well without directly calling them out as members of the military community.

- Schools should always be prepared for the unexpected, and that is especially important in dealing with military-connected children. Teachers, administrators, and counselors should have a plan in place to determine what they will do if a military-connected student in their school finds himself or herself dealing with a hardship that comes from growing up military, such as deployment orders, a new duty station, or anything else that can impact learning.
- In terms of modes, online learning might be difficult as computer communication is the primary mode used for deployed parents so they might have some hesitancy in wanting to be on the computer. Additionally, schools should allow for extra breaks and safe spaces within the school where military-connected adolescents can go if they are feeling as though they are overwhelmed because of the experiences as a forgotten conscript.
- Each school should partner with a mental health facility or with counselors who specialize in working with adolescents to make sure that they have someone they can seek help from if they find themselves out of their depth with military-connected students. There will be times when the trauma a forgotten conscript is dealing with is beyond what a school can help with, so they need to have someone or someplace to refer the parents where the student can get the help needed.
- Since military students move at a much higher rate than their civilian peers, it would be beneficial for the current school to contact the next one that the student will be attending to share valuable information about that child. This is especially helpful if the student has experienced some sort of trauma due to parental absence or tragedy during military conflict as the new school will already be aware and can start helping to support on day one.
- As already mentioned, the development and training of the staff *must* include evidence-based data and strategies on how to support, understand, work with, and teach military-connected children. They need to know how to recognize warning signs when a forgotten conscript is finding themselves feeling lost, isolated, or simply not their normal selves. They need to feel as though those trusted to educate them to understand them beyond just typical adolescent issues.

Of course, there is no one right way to approach teaching military-connected adolescents. Just like children that belong to other groups or cultures, there are norms and common occurrences, but each person may react to the stress of military life and experiences differently. A student's behavior might fluctuate and changes in attitude might occur as families go for long stretches without hearing from loved ones. Finding a way to reach out to military-connected adolescents with empathy and understanding can help military-connected adolescents flourish. Or not, if they continue to remain forgotten on education.

* * *

Although only nine forgotten conscripts were included in this book, their voices provide richness to the research concerning military-connected adolescents. They allowed the veil that hides their invisible culture from the world to be pulled back so we can take a gander and learn from them. They shared who they think they are, their achievements and successes, their losses and sorrows, their hopes and dreams. We should all be so brave.

Military-connected adolescents see themselves as confident, caring, and capable of handling nearly anything life has in store for them. They come from a childhood colored by high expectations, school struggles, relationships both strained and strengthened, parental absence, and the development of myriad coping strategies as the experiences they encounter endure long after they reach adulthood.

In a nation that has been at continuous war around the globe, where our country's fighting force needs to be in a prime position to defend this nation, ignoring the forgotten conscripts left behind seems indefensible.

Military-connected adolescents face obstacles and situations often unrivaled among their civilian counterparts. Their resiliency and ability to thrive is nothing short of inspirational. Perhaps one day these forgotten conscripts will no longer be overlooked, nor will the gratitude for the role they play in supporting our fighting forces be invisible.

This is an attempt to make visible my own gratitude for their service.

Glossary of Common Military Terms and Acronyms

As with any group, there is a lexicon used that only makes sense to those who hold membership within the group. Below is a list of terms and acronyms from the *DoD Dictionary of Military and Associated Terms* (2021) often used within this culture—including by forgotten conscripts—that should be known and understood by teachers and administrators of military-connected students:

AAFES—Army and Air Force Exchange Service. Also referred to as the PX or Post Exchange.

active duty—Full-time duty in the active military service of the United States, including active duty or full-time training duty in the Reserve Component.

Active Guard and Reserve—National Guard and Reserve members who are on voluntary active duty providing full-time support to National Guard, Reserve, and Active Component organizations to organize, administer, recruiting, instructing, or training the Reserve Components.

alert order—1. A planning directive normally associated with a crisis, issued by the Chairman of the Joint Chiefs of Staff, on behalf of the President or Secretary of Defense, that provides essential planning guidance and directs the development, adaptation, or refinement of a plan/order after the directing authority approves a military course of action. 2. A planning directive that provides essential planning guidance, directs the initiation of planning after the directing authority approves a military course of action but does not authorize execution.

Armed Forces of the United States—A term used to denote collectively all components of the Army, Marine Corps, Navy, Air Force, and Coast Guard (when mobilized under Title 10, United States Code, to augment the Navy).

ASVAB—Armed Services Vocational Aptitude Battery. Given to civilians before enlistment into the military.

AWOL—Absent without Leave for soldiers who leave or fail to report as directed. Can result in a term of imprisonment.

BAH—Basic allowance for housing; helps with the cost of housing for those not living on base.

BAS—Basic allowance for subsistence; helps with the cost of food for those not living on base.

base—1. A locality from which operations are projected or supported. 2. An area or locality containing installations that provide logistics or other support. 3. Home airfield or home carrier. Also referred to as a facility, post, or joint base if more than one military branch is working together.

battalion—Unit of 300–1,000 soldiers.

BCT—Basic combat training; initial training for all newly enlisted soldiers in all branches of the military.

BDU—Basic dress uniform; the assigned or required uniform of a military soldier. Each branch has its own required uniform for soldiers.

branch—1. A subdivision of any organization. 2. A geographically separate unit of an activity, which performs all or part of the primary functions of the parent activity on a smaller scale. 3. An arm or service of the Army.

brigade—Unit of 3,000–5,000 soldiers.

campaign—A series of related operations aimed at achieving strategic and operational objectives within a given time and space.

casualty—Any person who is lost to the organization by having been declared dead, duty status—whereabouts unknown, missing, ill, or injured. Also used with *casualty evacuation* and *casualty rate*.

chain of command—The succession of commanding officers from a superior to a subordinate through which command is exercised.

civil affairs—Designated Active Component and Reserve Component forces and units organized, trained, and equipped specifically to conduct civil affairs operations and to support civil-military operations. Also used with civil service.

CO—Commanding officer.

command—1. The authority that a commander in the armed forces lawfully exercises over subordinates by rank or assignment. 2. An order given by a commander; that is, the will of the commander expressed to bring about a particular action. 3. A unit or units, an organization, or an area under the command of one individual.

company—Unit of 60–200 soldiers.

CONUS—Continental United States; does not include bases in overseas locations.

course of action—1. Any sequence of activities that an individual or unit may follow. 2. A scheme developed to accomplish a mission.

delayed entry program—A program under which an individual may enlist in a Reserve Component of a Service and specify a future reporting date for entry on active duty that would coincide with the availability of training spaces and with personal plans. Often used by those still in school (secondary or college).

demobilization—1. The process of transitioning a conflict or wartime military establishment and defense-based civilian economy to a peacetime configuration while maintaining national security and economic vitality. 2. The process necessary to release from active duty, or federal service, units, and Reserve Component members who were ordered to active duty or called to federal service.

dependents—An employee's spouse; children who are unmarried and under age 21 years or who, regardless of age, are physically or mentally incapable of self-support; dependent parents, including step and legally adoptive parents of the employee's spouse; and dependent brothers and sisters, including step and legally adoptive brothers and sisters of the employee's spouse who are unmarried and under 21 years of age or who, regardless of age, are physically or mentally incapable of self-support.

deployment—The movement of forces into and out of an operational area. Also used with *deployment order* or *deployment planning*.

DFAC—Dining facility on a military base.

double-time—Used with military communication to indicate the receiver should do a specific task at a fast rate or pace.

downrange—Military colloquialism referring to a conflict region or war zone.

division—Unit of 10,000–15,000 soldiers.

DoD—Department of Defense, often used in conjunction with DoD schools, which are only open to military-connected children.

E—Enlisted soldier with a rank of E-4 or below.

engagement—1. An attack against an air or missile threat. (JP 3–01) 2. A tactical conflict, usually between opposing lower echelons maneuver forces. Also referred to as a *battle* or *campaign*.

exercise—A military maneuver or simulated wartime operation involving planning, preparation, and execution that is carried out for the purpose of training and evaluation.

FEMA—Federal Emergency Management Agency (DHS)

family readiness—The state of being prepared to effectively navigate the challenges of daily living experienced in the unique context of military service, including mobility and financial readiness, mobilization and deployment readiness, and personal and family life readiness.

FSA—Family separation allowance; provided to families when the soldier is given an unaccompanied tour of duty orders to a location where the family cannot move.

go/no-go—A critical point at which a decision to proceed or not must be made.

homeland—The physical region that includes the continental United States, Alaska, Hawaii, United States territories, and surrounding territorial waters and airspace. Also used with homeland defense and homeland security.

inactive duty training—Authorized training performed by a member of a Reserve Component, not on active duty or active duty for training and consisting of regularly scheduled unit training assemblies, additional training assemblies, periods of appropriate duty or equivalent training, and any special additional duties authorized for Reserve Component personnel by the Secretary concerned, and performed by them in connection with the prescribed activities of the organization in which they are assigned with or without pay.

Individual Ready Reserve—A manpower pool consisting of individuals who have had some training or who have served previously in the Active Component or in the Selected Reserve and may have some period of their military service obligation remaining. Also referred to as IRR.

KIA—Killed in action

logistics—Planning and executing the movement and support of forces.

maneuver—1. A movement to place ships, aircraft, or land forces in a position of advantage over the enemy. 2. A tactical exercise carried out at sea, in the air, on the ground, or a map in imitation of war. 3. The operation of a ship, aircraft, or vehicle to cause it to perform desired movements. 4. Employment of forces in the operational area, through movement in combination with fires and information, to achieve a position of advantage in respect to the enemy. Also referred to as a mission or operation.

MEPS—Medical entrance processing station; initial processing for new soldiers and also to receive new soldiers on base.

MHA—Military housing allowance or military housing area on base.

MIA—Missing in action.

mobilization—1. The process of assembling and organizing national resources to support national objectives in times of war or other emergencies. See also industrial mobilization. 2. The process by which the Armed Forces of the United States, or part of them, are brought to a state of readiness for war or other national emergencies. Also referred to as MOB or industrial mobilization.

morale, welfare, and recreation—The merging of multiple unconnected disciplines into programs that improve unit readiness; promote fitness; build unit morale and cohesion; enhance the quality of life; and provide recreational, social, and other support services. Also referred to as MWR.

MOS—Military occupational specialty; each branch has its own MOS list as each branch serves its own role in supporting the armed forces.

national emergency—A condition declared by the President or Congress by powers previously vested in them that authorize certain emergency actions to be undertaken in the national interest.

national security—A collective term encompassing both national defense and foreign relations of the United States to gain: a. A military or defense advantage over any foreign nation or group of nations; b. A favorable foreign relations position; or c. A defense posture capable of successfully resisting hostile or destructive action from within or without, overt or covert.

NCO—Non-commissioned officer; an enlisted soldier with the rank of E-4 or above.

need to know—A criterion used in security procedures that requires the custodians of classified information to establish, before disclosure, that the intended recipient must have access to the information to perform his or her official duties.

O—An officer in the military who serves in a leadership capacity over enlisted soldiers after completion of OCS.

objective—1. The clearly defined, decisive, and attainable goal toward which an operation is directed. 2. The specific goal of the action taken is essential to the commander's plan. Also referred to as *targets*.

obligation—The time frame in which a civilian agrees to serve as a soldier featuring a combination of active duty and reserves duty.

OCONUS—Outside of the continental United States; all military bases in overseas locations.

OCS—Officer candidate school; program for soldiers to become officers in the military.

operations security—A capability that identifies and controls critical information, indicators of friendly force actions attendant to military operations, and incorporates countermeasures to reduce the risk of an adversary exploiting vulnerabilities. Also referred to as OPSEC.

PCS—Permanent change of station, often as a result of military orders.

PFT—Physical fitness test, given at regular intervals with various requirements based upon age, gender, and branch of service.

POW—Prisoner of war.

preventive maintenance—Care and service of equipment and facilities in satisfactory operating condition by systematic inspection, detection, and correction of incipient failures either before they occur or before they develop into major defects.

PT—Physical training, often done as a company, at regular intervals depending on the branch of service.

PTSD—Post-traumatic stress disorder.

public affairs—Communication activities with external and internal audiences.

R&R—Rest and recuperation, often given to soldiers during and/or after deployment, tour of duty, or other training.

rank—The grade or standing of a soldier in the military often broken down into enlisted and officer.

readiness—The ability of military forces to fight and meet the demands of assigned missions.

reception—1. All ground arrangements are connected with the delivery and disposition of air or sea drops. 2. Arrangements to welcome and provide secure quarters or transportation for defectors, escapees, evaders, or incoming agents.

reintegrate—In personnel recovery, the task of providing medical care and psychological decompression to allow the conduct of appropriate debriefings to ultimately return recovered personnel back to duty and their family.

Reserve Component—The Armed Forces of the United States Reserve Component consists of the Army National Guard of the United States, the Army Reserve, the Navy Reserve, the Marine Corps Reserve, the Air National Guard of the United States, the Air Force Reserve, and the Coast Guard Reserve.

roger—Used with military communication to indicate one has received a message and understands it.

standard operating procedure—A set of instructions applicable to those features of operations that lend themselves to a definite or standardized procedure without loss of effectiveness. Also referred to as an SOP.

TDY—Temporary duty station for soldiers given unaccompanied orders for a short time frame, often less than six months.

tour of duty—A period in service for a specific duty tour.

tracking—Used in communication, often in the form of a question such as, "Are you tracking?," to ensure the receiver of the message is understanding what is being relayed.

TRICARE—Military health care program provided to soldiers and their dependents.

wounded warrior programs—A system of support and advocacy to guide and assist the wounded, ill, and injured Service members and family or designated caregiver through treatment, rehabilitation, return to duty, or military retirement into the civilian community. Each Military Department has a unique wounded warrior program that addresses its Service members' needs.

References

Astor, R. A., Jacobson, L., & Benbenishty, R. (2015). *The school administrator's guide for supporting students from military families*. Teachers College Press.

Atuel, H., Esqueda, M., & Jacobson, L. (2011). The military child within the public school education system. *Los Angeles, CA: USC Center for Innovation and Research on Veterans & Military Families*.

Baptist, J., Barros, P., Cafferky, B., & Johannes, E. (2015). Resilience building among adolescents from national guard families: Applying a developmental contextual model. *Journal of Adolescent Research, 30*(3), 306–334. https://doi-org.ezproxy.lib.ou.edu/10.1177/0743558414558592

Blum, R. (2005). *Best practices: Building blocks for enhancing school environment* [Monograph Series]. *Johns Hopkins University, Bloomberg School of Public Health Military Child Initiative* . Retrieved from http://www.jhsph.edu/research/centers-and-institutes/military-child-initiative/resources/Best_Practices_monograph.pdf.

Bolton, A. (2006). Deployment disruptions. *On the Move, 6*(3), 32–34.

Bradshaw, C. P., Sudhinaraset, M., Mmari, K., & Blum, R. W. (2010). School transitions among military adolescents: A qualitative study of stress and coping. *School Psychology Review, 39*(1), 84–105.

Chandra, A., & London, A. S. (2013). Unlocking insights about military children and families. *The Future of Children, 23*(2), 187–198.

Chandra, A., Martin, L. T., Hawkins, S. A., & Richardson, A. (2010). The impact of parental deployment on child social and emotional functioning: Perspectives of school staff. *Journal of Adolescent Health, 46*(3), 218–223.

Chartrand, M. M., & Siegel, B. (2007). At war in Iraq and Afghanistan: Children in US military families. *Academic Pediatrics, 7*(1), 1–2.

Clever, M., & Segal, D. R. (2013). The demographics of military children and families. *The Future of Children, 23*(2), 13–39.

De Pedro, K. T., Astor, R. A., Gilreath, T. D., Benbenishty, R., & Berkowitz, R. (2018). School climate, deployment, and mental health among students in military-connected schools. *Youth & Society, 50*(1), 93–115. https://doi-org.ezproxy.lib.ou.edu/10.1177/0044118X15592296

DoD Dictionary of Military and Associated Terms (2021). Retrieved on July 11, 2021, from https://www.jcs.mil/Portals/36/Documents/Doctrine/pubs/dictionary.pdf

Easterbrooks, M. A., Ginsburg, K., & Lerner, R. M. (2013). Resilience among military youth. *The Future of children, 23*(2), 99–120.

Ender, M. G. (2005). Military brats: Film representations of children from military families. *Armed Forces & Society, 32*(1), 24–43.

Engel, R. C., Gallagher, L. B., & Lyle, D. S. (2010). Military deployments and children's academic achievement: Evidence from Department of Defense Education Activity Schools. *Economics of Education Review, 29*(1), 73–82.

Erikson, E. H. (1968). *Identity: Youth and crisis* (No. 7). WW Norton & Company.

Esqueda, M. C., Astor, R. A., & De Pedro, K. M. T. (2012). A call to duty: Educational policy and school reform addressing the needs of children from military families. *Educational Researcher, 41*(2), 65–70.

Ginsburg, K. R., & Jablow, M. M. (2006). *Building resilience in children and teens*. American Academy of Pediatrics.

Hall, L. (2011). The importance of understanding military culture. *Social Work in Health Care*, 50(1), 4–18.

Harrison, J., & Vannest, K. J. (2008). Educators supporting families in times of crisis: Military reserve deployments. *Preventing School Failure: Alternative Education for Children and Youth, 52*(4), 17–24.

Hoersting, R. C., & Jenkins, S. R. (2011). No place to call home: Cultural homelessness, self-esteem and cross-cultural identities. *International Journal of Intercultural Relations, 35*(1), 17–30.

Huebner, A. J., Mancini, J. A., Bowen, G. L., & Orthner, D. K. (2009). Shadowed by war: Building community capacity to support military families. *Family Relations, 58*(2), 216–228.

Huebner, A. J., Mancini, J. A., Wilcox, R. M., Grass, S. R., & Grass, G. A. (2007). Parental deployment and youth in military families: Exploring uncertainty and ambiguous loss. *Family Relations, 56*(2), 112–122.

Hylmö, A. (2002). Other expatriate adolescents: A postmodern approach to understanding expatriate adolescents among non-US children. *Military brats and other global nomads: Growing up in organization families*, 193–210.

Jordan, K. A. F. (2002). Identity formation and the adult third culture kid. In Ender, M.G. (Eds.), *Military brats and other global nomads: Growing up in organization families* (211–228). Connecticut: Praeger Publications.

Knox, J., & Price, D. (1999). Total force and the new American military family: Implications for social work practice. *Families in Society: The Journal of Contemporary Social Services, 80*(2), 128–136.

Kranke, D. (2019). teachers' perspectives on educating military-connected students: The forgotten group. *Children & Schools, 41*(3), 189–190. https://doi-org.ezproxy.lib.ou.edu/10.1093/cs/cdz014

Kranke, D., Barmak, S., Weiss, E., & Dobalian, A. (2019). The application of a self-labeling approach among military-connected adolescents in a public school setting. *Health & Social Work, 44*(3), 193–201. https://doi-org.ezproxy.lib.ou.edu/10.1093/hsw/hlz007

Lester, P., & Flake, L. C. E. (2013). How wartime military service affects children and families. *The Future of Children, 23*(2), 121–141.

Lester, P., Peterson, K., Reeves, J., Knauss, L., Glover, D., Mogil, C., . . . & Beardslee, W. (2010). The long war and parental combat deployment: Effects on military children and at-home spouses. *Journal of the American Academy of Child & Adolescent Psychiatry, 49*(4), 310–320.

Litwack, L., & Foster, C. L. (1981). Isolation and identity: Loss in the military. *Journal of Counseling & Development, 59*(6), 386–388.

Masten, A. S. (2013). Afterword: What we can learn from military children and families. *The Future of Children*, 23(2), 199–212.

Masten, A. S., Best, K. M., & Garmezy, N. (1990). Resilience and development: Contributions from the study of children who overcome adversity. *Development and Psychopathology, 2*(4), 425–444.

McCarthy, N. (2015, June 23). The World's Biggest Employers. *Forbes*. Retrieved on August 27, 2018 from https://www.forbes.com/sites/niallmccarthy/2015/06/23/the-worlds-biggest-employers-infographic/#5cb4dce8686b

McCubbin, H. I., Dahl, B., & Hunter, E. (1976). Research on the military family: A review. In McCubbin, H. I., Dahl, B., & Hunter, E. (Eds.), *Families in the military system*, (291–319). Thousand Lakes, CA: SAGE Publications.

McDonald, K. E. (2010). Transculturals: Identifying the invisible minority. *Journal of Multicultural Counseling and Development, 38*(1), 39–50.

Memorandum of understanding between Department of Defense and Department of Education. (2008). Retrieved from Department of Defense Education Activity website: http://www.dodea.edu/Partnership/upload/reference-mou.pdf.

Milburn, N. G., & Lightfoot, M. (2013). Adolescents in wartime US military families: A developmental perspective on challenges and resources. *Clinical Child & Family Psychology Review*, 16(3), 266–277. doi:10.1007/s10567-013-0144-0

Military Leadership Diversity Commission. (2009, December). Department of defense core values. Retrieved from http://diversity.defense.gov/Portals/51/Documents/Resources/Commission/docs/Issue%20Papers/Paper%2006%20-%20DOD%20Core%20Values.pdf.

Mmari, K., Roche, K. M., Sudhinaraset, M., & Blum, R. (2009). When a parent goes off to war: Exploring the issues faced by adolescents and their families. *Youth & Society, 40*(4), 455–475.

Montalvo, P. (1976). Family separation in the army: a study of the problems encountered and the caretaking resources used by career army families undergoing military separation. In McCubbin, H. I., Dahl, B., & Hunter, E. (Eds.), *Families in the military system*, (42–66). Thousand Lakes, CA: SAGE Publications.

Moore, A. M., & Barker, G. G. (2011). Confused or multicultural: Third culture individuals' cultural identity. *International Journal of Intercultural Relations, 36*(4), 553–562.

O'Leary, V. E., & Ickovics, J. R. (1995). Resilience and thriving in response to challenge: an opportunity for a paradigm shift in women's health. *Women's health (Hillsdale, NJ), 1*(2), 121–142.

Olsen, K. (2012). The hardest year: For blue star children, a parent's deployment brings a unique type of stress. *The American Legion Magazine, 172*(4), 26–32.

Park, N. (2011). Military children and families: Strengths and challenges during peace and war. *American Psychologist, 66*(1), 65–72.

Pollock, D., & Van Reken, R. (2009). *Third culture kids: Growing up among worlds.* Nicholas Brealey Publishing.

Scarf, D., Moradi, S., McGaw, K., Hewitt, J., Hayhurst, J. G., Boyes, M., . . . & Hunter, J. A. (2016). Somewhere I belong: Long-term increases in adolescents' resilience are predicted by perceived belonging to the in-group. *British Journal of Social Psychology, 55*(3), 588–599.

Schwartz, S. J., Donnellan, M. B., Ravert, R. D., Luyckx, K., & Zamboanga, B. L. (2012). Identity development, personality, and well-being in adolescence and emerging adulthood: Theory, research, and recent advances. In Weiner, I.B., Lerner, R.M., Easterbrooks, M.A. & Mistry, J. (Eds.), *Handbook of Psychology* (339–364). New Jersey: John Wiley & Sons, Inc.

Segal, M. W. (1986). The military and the family as greedy institutions. *Armed Forces & Society, 13*(1), 9–38.

Sherman, M. & Glenn, M.A. (2006). Opportunities for school psychologists working with children of military families. *On the Move, 6*(3), 40–45.

Stipek, D. 2006. Relationships matter. *Educational Leadership, 64*(1): 46–4s9.

Thompson, D. E., Baptist, J., Miller, B., & Henry, U. (2017). Children of the U.S. national guard: Making meaning and responding to parental deployment. *Youth & Society, 49*(8), 1040–1056.

Tyler, M. P. (2002). The military teenager in Europe: Perspectives for health care providers. *Military brats and other global nomads: Growing up in organization families*, 25–34.

Wertsch, M. E. (1991). *Military brats: Legacies of childhood inside the fortress.* New York: Harmony Books.

Williams, K. C., & Mariglia, L. L. (2002). Military brats: Issues and associations in adulthood. In Ender, M.G. (Eds.), *Military brats and other global nomads: Growing up in organization families* (67–82). Connecticut: Praeger Publications.

Williamson, V., Stevelink, S. A. M., Da Silva, E., & Fear, N. T. (2018). A systematic review of wellbeing in children: A comparison of military and civilian families. *Child and Adolescent Psychiatry and Mental Health, 12,* 46. https://doi-org.ezproxy.lib.ou.edu/10.1186/s13034-018-0252-1

About the Author

Born in a hospital just outside of Fort Stewart, Georgia, Dr. **Jennie L. Hanna** has proudly claimed the moniker military brat since childhood. Since then, she has claimed several other titles within the military culture: military soldier, Army wife, Air Force mom, and educator of thousands of forgotten conscripts.

Dr. Hanna earned her Ph.D. from the University of Oklahoma, where she focused on military culture and multicultural education in secondary schools. She has been an English educator in Fort Sill, Oklahoma, for the past 13 years in both high school and collegiate classrooms.